Anger Management

Coleman Christy Tanos

Published by Coleman Christy, 2023.

While every precaution has been taken in the preparation of this book, the publisher assumes no responsibility for errors or omissions, or for damages resulting from the use of the information contained herein.

ANGER MANAGEMENT

First edition. December 27, 2023.

ISBN: 979-8223895114

Written by Coleman Christy Tanos.

ANGER MANAGEMENT

****

Anger as Emotion: the Best Tips to Learn how to Manage it.
Exercises for Emotions Self-control
By: **Coleman Christy Tano**

— —

Copyright 2023; Coleman Christy Tano All Rights Reserved.

INTRODUCTION

To excel in life and achieve all your goals, you must possess the correct mindset. You can and will accomplish so much more when you have an attitude or mind that expects success. Learn the secrets to unlocking the door to unlimited success and achievement through developing mental toughness

If you want to learn the quality of self-control and mental toughness read this book.

Developing mental toughness is not easy. However, with the right information and a motivation to succeed, you will be able to develop this through your own efforts.

The world is filled with temptation. It is so irresistible. we can be tempted to spend too much money, to cheat, to overeat or drink too much. Resisting temptation is never easy, it tries to tell us that we MUST do something that we might not otherwise do. Self control is one of the MUST have in order to help us to fight and overcome temptation. Studies has shown that we humans can indeed improve our ability to have self-control. In order to master self-control, a person must have the ability to do abstract thinking and to psychologically distance himself from the situation.

Let's say that you have a plan to become successful in your career. Therefore, any thoughts or actions that run contrary to your mission must be extinguished. You must work to maintain self-control to meet the standard that you have set for yourself. If you want to learn the quality of self-control, read this chapter. A lack of self-control is good, once admitted to. If your life is becoming unmanageable there is hope. This book discusses causes and solutions to Self-control & Mental Toughness, how to boost your Willpower and Self-discipline to achieve a Champion's mindset.

This book will also discuss the benefits of possessing a mental toughness, by providing you with some mental strength tips that will enable you to meet and overcome all challenges you face in life.

Before you can have sufficient Positive self control over your life, you need to have a fresh revelation in the study of what you are actually trying to get under control, which is your soul first, then the easy part your body.

Some psychologists believe that self-control is a limited resource. What they are saying is that every person has only a certain amount of self-control to use each day. Once it's used up, you might as well go to bed, or you can forget resisting that chocolate chip cookie dough ice cream in the freezer.

Here is an example. Studies have shown that people who exercise in the morning are more likely to succeed. They succeed, in part, because they haven't had to use up any self-control. This fresh supply of self-control gives them the energy to resist the temptation to skip the workout.

Everyone has their moments which leaves them wondering or remarking that they could have handled a situation better. Those are the times when we lose our self-control and it seems we just have no idea how it happened or why we did what we did. Achieving self-control is a critical ingredient in achieving success in whatever facet of society we partake in. It can mean the difference between making a good impression or making a terrible one, it can literally change how people perceive you depending on how you are able to handle your self-control.

In the morning we wake up and one of the important things we do is the mirror activity. We observe our selves so that we can be better prepared to interact with society. This is the same principle in that we need to observe our own character, beliefs and actions so that we can be sure that we are really prepared to have that self-control.

Each one of us has the ability to achieve great self-control which can catapult us to greatness, after all greatness is not copyrighted to anyone. It is up to us to see the greatness within ourselves and self-control is that fist step towards achieving that.

When it comes to certain people some are born mentally tough and others are not. Does this mean that if you are one of the people that aren't born mentally tough that you can never get tough? The answer is no.

What people don't realize is that mental toughness can be built, gained or learned. The only advantage you have when you are born tough is that you won't have to work as hard to keep it or build up its level.

Getting mentally tougher is like working out your muscles. If you lift weights all the time then you are going to get stronger. The reason that you get strong is because your muscles respond to the lifting of the weights. In much of the same manner that you can work out your mind and make it tougher.

That is all well and go, but how does one make it tougher and how long will it take? Unfortunately, it can take some time and it won't be the easiest thing in the world to do but it is completely possible. The best way to make yourself mentally tougher is to step out side of your comfort zone as often as you can, by doing this you are testing the limits of what you think you can and can't do.

An example of this would be in an martial arts practice. Pushing yourself when you are tired, want to stop or think you can't handle it any more are perfect examples. If you have practiced so hard that you think you can't move a muscle and can't continue one more minute, than pushing yourself to continue is the way to become more mentally tough.

Working through pain is another example of mental toughness. I want to note though, that pain can signify that something is quite wrong and you should get it looked at. There is a difference of being hurt and being injured.

Being hurt is nothing serious and you can continue to work out. For example, you might be hurt if your muscles are sore from lifting the day before, or if you have a headache. These, while annoying, will not cause any serious harm and will help you build mental toughness. Being injured on the other hand, are things along the lines of breaking a bone, tearing muscles, or having a concussion. All are serious in nature and should be immediately checked out.

So remember that mental toughness can be built. It can be built by getting out of your own comfort zone and pushing through fatigue, doubt, and pain.

You will learn how to:

boost your Willpower and Self-discipline to achieve a Champion's mindset.

The ultimate guide to learn how to develop powerful Daily Habits to Program Your Mind, Build Mental strength, Self-Confidence and Grit.

Re-program your subconscious mind

Set action steps and definitive goals

Manage and utilize your emotions

Recognize the skills you need to begin building to achieve success

Manage your time and increase your productivity

Control your thoughts and develop an unstoppable mindset

Make better decisions, even if under pressure.

Keep yourself focused on your goals, even between distractions.

Boos your leadership skills

Develop your willpower and connection with your spiritual self.

Use your mind to its full potential.

Reach incredible levels of self-discipline in your life to become relentless.

Fix your emotional weakness

Reach long-term perseverance.
Transform your body and mind.

CHAPTER 1

SELF CONTROL

Self-control is defined as "control of oneself" or the "ability to master one's desires and impulses. Interestingly, self-control is actually perceived in several ways. Philosophically speaking self-control could be described as the exertion of one's own will. Psychologically, self-control usually refers to a person's self-perception, belief system, as well as the ability to set boundaries on their own behavior. Among some scientific communities, the issue seems to be whether or not what we perceive as "normal" (and hence the standard that the person lacking self-control violates) is truly an accurate setting to work with. Most people assume that self-control is healthier than impulsiveness. However, this has to be compared to each person's value system. For example, some communities may demand stringent behavior as regards sexual morality. Other communities will hold that generosity and pacifism are more important than law. Then some communities will stress that allegiance to a mission is what is truly righteous. Which of the communities has the highest standard of morality?

Knowing what you know about these various communities, how can you determine if a member truly loses self-control and if it's harmful to their well being? The answer is not a dogmatic one; it's simply that if the member chooses to adhere to a belief system (or desires to live in only one of the communities) then their level of self-control must be in accordance with the community's. This way, they feel no personal guilt nor does he offend other members of the community. Now how does this apply in a professional context, specifically, to one individual?

If you are a self-starting businessperson or have an artistically driven mind, then you may not feel as if you belong to any community. Your concern is not with morals but with success. So how does the concept of self-control fit into this equation? First, understand that everyone has a system of belief. Nobody truly believes in nothing;

otherwise, that person would live entirely on animalistic instinct. All human beings (even the slow ones that repeatedly get ticketed for drunk driving) have logical thought processes. Hence, we all have a system of belief. Before you analyze what self-control means to you, you must first analyze what you believe. You are your own community and you set the guidelines as to what is right or wrong, productive or unproductive.

Let's say that you have a plan to become successful in your career. This is the mission of your self-contained community. Therefore, any thoughts or actions that run contrary to your mission must be extinguished. This is not to suggest that fascism or communism in real life is right or wrong. After all, when you are discussing government you must take into account the lives of many, as opposed to just one. However, when you are a self-starter, then you are in charge of all your faculties and must have them work for you, not independently of you. Sometimes people do require rigid structure in their life in order to get things done. If you are naturally inclined to take it easy, if you tend to procrastinate, or if you are easily distracted from completing a simple goal,

then these are disruptive factors in your community. You must work to maintain self-control to meet the standard that you have set for yourself.

If you find that procrastinating slows down your mission, or that watching television alters your set schedule, then you may have to use coercive techniques in order to train your body and mind. Science supports this theory, as even some highly intelligent people have been shown to lack motivation, especially when it comes to certain tasks. If you are a creative type that despises logistical or mathematic work, or a convergent thinker who has trouble thinking outside the box, then this can be challenging to your mission. You may have to exercise self-control, ensuring that you do not drift away to other time-consuming hobbies or even resort to shelving the project indefinitely.

Self-control doesn't necessarily mean resisting something that is "wrong"; rather, it refers to taking steps to control one's own tendencies if they are observed to be counterproductive. If you want to learn the quality of self-control, first decide what your mission is and what would be the best way to learn positive qualities. It may help you to slow down your "intake" or "output" (whatever the problem is) rather than to quit suddenly. Don't underestimate the value of enlisting others to help you. When you are accountable to someone else, it helps. You may have to sacrifice certain things that you enjoy, whether it is time-consuming gadgets, hobbies or types of food and drink. Once you determine to follow your goal through you must make necessary changes. Last but not least, remember to analyze your results and find room for improvement. Celebrate your successes, no matter how small. It is about making progress in life that brings us the success we want and deserve.

Self-control is among the diverse categories of personal development. It is the actual ability to inspire yourself to choose the important things in your life and restrain from our animal-like desires. Yet, the foundation of this personal development is situated in a powerful perseverance and correcting of oneself. Self-control creates a type of self-confidence within us towards things that we believe are hard to accomplish. It creates some sort of drive connected with determination within us which make us attain our desired goals.

However, it is necessary that a good amount of relaxation be obtained to adequately implement self-control in our everyday life. A person needs to find ways to de-stress themselves. It can be by simply listening to music or work out along with other things that will enhance one's energy level. This will make it possible for the person to complete their task. For example, when there is a student who would like to finish a goal of finishing their entire study course in one day for a specific topic, then he would be studying the entire day. But, this could produce a lot of pressure for his mind and hinder his ability associated with learning. Therefore he might consider breaks in between to unwind himself, then this will decrease stress and increase efficiency.

Self-awareness will be the main factor that needs to be resolved for successful self-control. One should first examine one's personal character and figure out the strengths and weaknesses. Next, be ready to endure the temptation that you will face in your everyday life with regards to your weakness. For instance, lets say you like candy and you are used to having it every day, you will need to make efforts to limit it to only two times a week. This is one way you can strengthen yourself and contribute to your own personal development of self-control.

So we can say that self-control is really the ability to deny one's own temptation to a particular thing or even a task. This brings us to another part of self-control I.e. positive perseverance. Our commitment causes us to have a serious choice to accomplish a task. Most of us have the habit to make up our mind for a mission, but because of our laziness or wish for other comforts, we are not able to abide to it. The most typical example of this can be working out in the morning, which most of us usually stop simply because we don't want to give up our sleep. Here is where many of us clearly realize the heart and soul of a solid commitment. A person having a strong commitment will give up his conveniences and create his goal.

GAINING SELF CONTROL

Self control is a person's ability to control emotions, desires, and actions. It is the ability to separate the feelings from the self. When you let your feelings become you, your actions and decision making capabilities become hindered. This may lead to you reacting based on your feelings and not acting according to the situation. It takes a lot of practice and effort to gain control over your feelings. But all that effort and practice will pay off in the long run and pave the way for your success in leading a well balanced life.

Needs are different from desires — thereare times when desires become so strong that they transform into needs. Self control will keep those desires under control. Think of your favorite food, or even better bring it home and don't eat it yet. As a first step to self control set your mind that you will not eat that food for 'x' number of days. I know, this sounds kind of ridiculous, but trust me it works. Abstaining from something that you really crave for will develop resistance to impulses and desires in you. When you can resist temptation you have gained control over your desires.

All our actions are defined by our emotions. Emotions are the most difficult to control, but if you can gain that control over your feelings you have mastered self control. Emotions could be anything ranging from anger, happiness, sorrow, frustration, etc. Out of all these the biggest step towards greater self control is controlling anger and frustration. Anger overpowers your mind and senses; you may do or say something that you will regret later. Anger is self-destructive, and you don't want to walk that path. When any person or situation makes you angry/frustrated, try this: Count till 3 before you react or divert your attention to anything that will give the required pause before reacting. This pause will mellow down your anger, and as you keep practicing you will eventually gain complete control over your temper.

Meditation is one of the best techniques to gain self control and balance your body and mind. Meditation helps unclutter your mind of unwanted thoughts and emotions and also helps you focus and de-stress. Having a calm and clear mind enables you to control your feelings and in turn your actions.

CHAPTER 2

15

SELF CONTROL AND DISCIPLINE

Have you ever wondered how other people seem to achieve more but yet you work just as hard? Have you ever wondered how others seem to be more successful and you know that you are just as intelligent, just as capable but yet for some reason you aren't doing as well?

There could be one key ingredient that you are missing to achieving your goals. It is an ingredient that is often taken for granted and overlooked because it is so simple and that is "self discipline".

What is self discipline?

It is the ability to do what you should do when you should do it whether you feel like it or not.

This is a quality you need to posses while on your journey to reaching your destination. Without it, you will struggle in reaching your goal.

What has been holding you back?

Before you can begin thinking about how to improve your self discipline, you need ask yourself what has been holding you back. This will give you a better idea of your thought processes, your beliefs, your behaviours and what action you can take to empower yourself to make positive changes.

So here are some questions I would like you to consider:

Why aren't you as successful as you would like to be?

What beliefs do you think have been disempowering you?

What behaviours do you think you could improve on?

Here are some other questions to consider?

Do you make excuses or procrastinate?

Are unclear and aren't sure of what you really want?

Do you think you deserve those rewards or are you unconsciously sabotaging your potential to achieve your goals?

Is there some part of you that believes you aren't capable? Or maybe all of the above are just excuses. Here is a secret to making that big change in your life... stop making excuses.

You can either have REASONS or you can have RESULTS! Which one do you chose?

Are you clear on what you want?

Before we start planning on what actions we can take to move in the right direction, we need to be clear on what that direction is, therefore it is imperative that you understand what success means to you. Everyone has their own definition of success and it doesn't make you right or wrong. It is what works for you and is based on your values. Is it about living up to your own expectations not someone else's?

So here are 3 more questions for you:

What does it mean for you to be successful? What does it look like?

Who are your role models when you think of success?

What characteristics do your role models possess? Or what is it about them that make them successful?

What does success mean to you?

Here are some ideas of what my students have told me success means to them:

Being able to live in your own way doing what you want to do

Being the person you want to be

Achieving the goals you set for yourself

To be happy and settle for what you want and not for any less

Feeling satisfied and fulfilled

To reach success, does it mean that everything has to be perfect? No, because success is about growth and progression. It doesn't have to be static - it can change.

What does it take to be a successful person? Here are some characteristics I believe successful people tend to possess. They are disciplined and they manage their time and actions effectively.

Long term thinkers and planners are willing to make sacrifices and delay gratification

Investing in continual learning - they make a habit of doing what unsuccessful people don't want to do.

Are you capable of adopting these qualities? Of course you are. You probably already do in the areas you are successful in but need to improve on them in areas you are still working on achieving. For example - maybe your finances are perfect because you save and manage your budget but your weight isn't ideal because you aren't investing time in consistently exercising.

Self discipline is necessary for success in order not to give into temptations. And our two greatest temptations are:

- The path of least resistance, and
- The expediency factor.

It is not our fault. We are all human and they are our weaknesses. We need to be disciplined enough to see past that and aim for RESULTS... otherwise all you have left are REASONS.

The good news is you can achieve almost any goal you set for yourself if you have self discipline. The even better news is self discipline can be learned.

If self-discipline is the key to success then the lack of self discipline is the key to failure.

Why are habits important to achieving success?

Whatever you do becomes a habit and habits can be hard to break.

They say it takes 21 days to create a habit so the trick is to start doing something/one thing, every day, and after 21 days it will feel weird not to do it. It is your job to refuse to act in any other way that is different to the good habit you are trying to create.

What are the results in achieving success?

You may have not thought of this, but what do you think happens when you start doing things that move you closer to achieving your success? What do you think happens to your self esteem? When you follow through with what you set out to do - don't you think you strengthen your trust with yourself? You will feel better about yourself

You will feel more confident

You will have more pride and self respect

You will most probably be willing to try more things because you have proven how capable and disciplined you really are and as an overall result you end up achieving more success!

Sounds like a fair trade to me.

You can apply self discipline in any area you want including health, work, finances, relationships, family and education.

simple steps to help you be more disciplined:

Decide and be clear on what you want. You must set achievable goals.

Determine what price you are willing to pay, that is, what habits are you willing to change? It's the bad habits that get in the way of self discipline. Be specific about what you are going to do differently on a daily basis. Write it down. Also write down your "what ifs" if you do stray.

Plan the day's activities in advance. If you're not used to planning then start simple. The night before, write down five things that you want to accomplish the next day. Then the next day mark them off as you do them - this is basic self discipline. It's also forming new good habits and tracking progress.

Resolve to be willing to pay the price. Take action and do it, and reward yourself for self-discipline accomplishments but make sure you chose rewards that help you move forward, not go backwards. Eg if you are trying to lose weight, don't make food your reward.

Model people who are already successful in the field you want to be successful in

Be a lifelong student of your craft - you can only get better. Don't fall into the trap of believing that you already know everything because "you really don't know what you don't know"

Put a plan of action in place to address temptations when they creep in, because they will always creep in and test you

Draw on your successes. Think about what you have achieved before to remind yourself how capable you are so that you don't lose your steam Put it in writing, andTake time to reflect daily. This is not a set and forget exercise

In a lot of ways, self-control is similar to mildness. But there is one key difference. Developing mildness will essentially keep you cool while maneuvering your way through life's inevitable stresses, and doing so requires a level of self-control, so the two qualities are linked. But there are times when even the mildest of people will run into a situation that pushes them toward - or over - the edge.

At that point, only a deep-seated self-control will prevent full-on meltdown from occurring. Self-control is really seated in the realization and appreciation of the fact that freaking out about a situation rarely if ever improves or solves it. It relies on a strong inner confidence that you're capable of handling any situation you come across and facing any stress successfully as long as you maintain control of your reactions to the extent that you can think before you act.

The greatest challenge we will face in life - in fact, the very purpose of our existence - is to learn how to overcome the natural tendencies within us and to develop self-control and discipline mentally, physically, emotionally, socially, morally, financially, and spiritually.

The difficulty of this necessary task should suggest the importance of the effort - for all things worthwhile require great work, discipline, and persistence. It is important to remember that the laws that govern self-control and discipline are the very same laws that dictate and determine success - namely: desire, belief, commitment, an organized plan, daily action, learn from and not repeat mistakes, persistence, and to never give up!

The next and most important principle to understand and implement into our lives is the reality that we literally are the 'master of [our] fate, the captain of [our] soul.' (William Ernest Henley). The greatest mystery, and most important task in life is to learn how to completely control our thoughts in such a way that they dictate our actions - actions that are good, disciplined, uplifting, and unselfish. And regardless of the constant daily bombardment of temptations, lusts, idleness, selfish pursuits, and natural tendencies that require no discipline - we must never give excuses and we absolutely must daily put forth effort. Is it difficult? Every day! Is it possible? Absolutely!

Success can only be found by design.

This is because you first have to determine what success is to you. You see success has a different measure for everyone. The biggest attribute that successful people have aside from the burning desire to succeed is self control and discipline. When we possess self control and discipline the bumps in the road are just that. Bumps. It's about the end result. Isn't life about the journey? Your right, it is. I put it back in your lap and state that if we do not have goals and aspirations that we are working toward we are just spectators in life. Do you want to succeed at life or watch other people succeed? What kind of life journey is sitting on the coach with the remote control and a bowl of popcorn? I have a fun saying I like to use in coaching sessions to lighten things up. "You have to go through it to get there."

MENTAL TOUGHNESS

We all experience frustration when our needs, wants and demands are not met, or when we are faced with obstacles that impede our progress. Frustration is a fact of life; therefore our ability to tolerate frustration is crucial to the successful achievement of our long-term goals.

When we are easily frustrated and upset, we are said to have, Low Frustration Tolerance . If, on the other hand, we are less disturbed or upset by short-term frustrations, and persevere through difficulties, we are said to have High Frustration Tolerance . Developing High Frustration Tolerance is vital to good mental health and a key element of Mental Toughness.

We all know that in our everyday lives, we will face obstacles, difficulties and hassles. People will let us down, trains won't run, cars won't start, we will have to queue and wait to be served, items will be out of stock and call centres will be busy. Amazingly enough, we habitually demand that these things do not happen, and that life should always be... the way we want it... easy, fast and without any hassle. So we may often complain, bleat, moan and rage. We may cry and whine that we are being "stressed out" or scream that we can't stand it! The psychologist, Albert Ellis, called this can't-stand-it-itis.

Having Mental Toughness means, that we must accept responsibility for our thoughts, emotions and behaviour. If we have Low Frustration Tolerance it is within our power and within our control to change the beliefs that cause us to feel frustrated.

You will achieve great results through developing mental toughness. So what is mental toughness? It is the desire of taking control of your emotions in performance situations. Some people claim that they work well under pressure. My mentors often argue that the statement is a myth, and pressure can actually hurt you. With added pressure, the chances are high that you will start having negative self-talk, and then lose belief in your ability to complete a task or project.

Some people appear to perform well under pressure. While a number of people may perceive some situations as pressure filled, the person who seems to perform well has a different perception on the level of threat of that particular situation. In other words, they excel under stressful situations because they can control their self-perception of it. That is, they learn to control their emotions because they have developed mental toughness.

Everyone is born with mental toughness, but how do you go about developing mental toughness? While some may not believe they were born with it, picture yourself in the following scenario. Suppose you had a bad day at work, and the only thing you can think about are the numerous problems stacked on top of one another. Your mind is scattered all over the place, and you don't seem to have a clue where your life is headed. Let's say you're driving, and as you approach home, you see a house on fire. You notice that it's your house burning down. You try to get close, but the fireman won't let you through. You're told it's too dangerous, but you know your kids are in there. What would you do? I'm sure you would choose to ignore the firemen and fight your way through the fire and do whatever you can to get the kids out. Your mind forgets everything else and you lose all your fears because your mind is so laser focused on bringing your kids to safety.

This is called mental toughness, where you focus all your energy and attention on one single task. So if we're born with mental toughness, why isn't everyone achieving great results? The problem is that most people have no clue what they want, or a compelling enough reason to fight for it, just like trying to save your kids from a burning house. They are not developing mental toughness. Mental energy is scattered all over the place, and they watch life go by instead of living it.

So if you truly want to achieve great things, you need to decide what you really want and why you want it. Uncover the emotional fire within, and convert that fire into motivation that will propel you to take the necessary steps to succeed. Ambition is not the only thing that fuels success, but it's the emotional power and feeling that you get from a winning experience. Take the time and think of what you really desire. If it doesn't excite you emotionally, then forget it. You need that emotion to sustain motivation and overcome obstacles that get in your way. Once you have this burning desire, you will start developing your mental toughness and stay laser focused on your goals.

"Concentration and mental toughness are the margins of victory", said Bill Russell. In fact, mental toughness is the most important ingredient that is very much necessary for achieving goals in life because during the course of your journey towards your life's goals, chances of you facing bumps are very high. Not only that, this trait will help you acquire resilience, determination and willpower so you can persist till you reach your goals.

Mental toughness gives you the ability and strength to push despite opposition and hurdles. So, it is imperative that you must try cultivating the trait. But before that, let us understand what we mean by mental toughness.

What is mental toughness?

Mental toughness can be described as the attribute that allows you to handle the difficulties you may face in your life. A few experts firmly restrict this attribute to the sports field. But a number of other experts believe that this attribute pervades every area of our life. Peter Clough and Dough Strycharczyk, researchers who authored the book "Developing Mental Toughness," says that this attribute is "the quality which determines in large part how people deal effectively with challenge, stressors, and pressure... irrespective of prevailing circumstances."

According to these researchers, this trait consists of a few critical components and they are challenge, control, commitment and confidence. As far as "challenge," the first component, is concerned, you must view challenges, not as obstacles, but as opportunities. The crux of "control," the second component, is to believe that you have complete control over your destiny and life.

Commitment is nothing but possessing the capabilities needed for sticking to tasks and ensuring to complete them regardless of the hurdles you may face. 'Confidence' is believing in your capabilities. Peter Clough and Dough Strycharczyk firmly say that mental toughness and the skills related to it apply to every area of life.

Researches prove that the attribute has a genetic link. At the same time, experts suggest that people can learn and strengthen their mental toughness as well. But how can you cultivate this trait?

1. Believe that you have the ability for achieving your goals

A study conducted in 2002 revealed that top performers and especially, elite athletes always possessed extreme self-belief. This means that they firmly believe that they can succeed. In other words, if you believe in yourself and keep encouraging yourself positively, you can achieve your goal regardless of what it is.

2. Prefer intrinsic motivations to external rewards

External rewards like popularity, money, etc. are certainly nice but intrinsic motivations are better because they come from the "within." This means you will love doing things just for doing them. When you love doing things, you will push harder and try to perform better. In fact, mentally tough people love doing things in which they are interested and their success in their tasks come from intrinsic motivations and not because of external rewards. This means that they love the challenges they may face while doing things and overcoming those challenges is the real reward for them.

3. Mentally tough people do not get upset when they encounter setbacks

Mentally tough people rebound even when they encounter setbacks and while doing so, they move ahead with stronger determination and resolve. They innovate to find out new ways for overcoming such phases.

4. They are self-directed

This means that they do not let things happen. Instead, they focus on creating the life they like to lead. They set goals and take appropriate action for going behind their goals and achieving them. In other words, they learn the process of setting goals and pursue the goals relentlessly.

5. They keep their focus even if there are distractions

Distractions are bound to be there in everyone's life but mentally tough people do not allow them to play spoil-sport to their focus. Remember that it is impossible to always have everything right. Even if other things need your attention, you must focus only on your goals and work towards achieving them.

6. They are committed

Commitment is a major ingredient that helps in cultivating mental toughness. Remember the words of Winston Churchill who said, "Success is not final, failure is not fatal: it is the courage to continue that counts." So, you should always remain committed to making the right efforts for achieving your goal

HOW TO BOOST YOUR WILLPOWER AND SELF-DISCIPLINE TO ACHIEVE A CHAMPION'S MINDSET.

Many of us associate the terms self discipline with images ranging from a grocery list to managing a giant construction project to memories of Mom and Dad trying to get us to conform to the norms of society. But what is self discipline really? And how does it relate to success? Why do so many of us perceive self discipline as something to be avoided, as if it was some kind of threat? A threat to what? Is there a part of us that suspects something that another part of us doesn't want to know about?

Aside from the whole multiple personality disorder aspect of these questions, if you go out on the street and ask people at random what they think self discipline is you are likely to get a stunning array of answers that reflect a broad range of perceptions of this concept. I believe that part of the reason why we respond to these terms in negative ways is that back when we were young and society was trying to get us to go along with its program, they used the concept of self-discipline to disguise the real process that was going on, which was more about social, economic and political indoctrination. After all, the system has to have drones.

There is something of genuine value here and to discover it we need to take a closer look at just what self discipline might actually be. One of the definitions of discipline in the dictionary is 'training that develops self control'. Training uses the power of conditioning to achieve its objectives, but what are we trying to achieve self control over? Our physical condition? Our quality of life? Our personality? Actually, there is only one place where self control occurs, in the mind. This is true because all things have their beginning as thoughts produced by either our conscious, unconscious or subconscious mind.

So when we talk about self discipline, that self is our mind and the discipline is over the activity of our mind. I realize that self-discipline of any kind is not exactly on everyone's 'gee I can't wait to do it' list and self discipline involving the mind is the last place we want to go rummaging around. Which in itself is strange in that it implies that there is something to fear in such an undertaking. Does the idea that we need to be afraid of our own mind sound a little sideways to you? The truth is, that this may be difficult but it is not impossible and we don't have to dig up traumatic experiences in order to develop the level of mental self control necessary to insure success in our lives. We just need to invest in a little focus and attention training.

We are talking about developing our ability to focus the attention of our mind and thereby develop our ability to concentrate on any given subject. Concentration develops contemplation and this is how we achieve a deep understanding of the subject we are focused on. This can get scary only when we choose a subject like self realization where we consciously seek to clean up our core belief system because it is a liability to us. But normally in the physical world we just need to develop more efficient thinking habits that allow us to perform more effectively and thereby achieve higher levels of success in the normal conduct of our lives.

Bringing the energy of our normally unruly mind's attention to one single point of focus is the goal and learning how to do this is the challenge. The absolute best way to develop mental self discipline in through the use of the main tool of the mental world, meditation. Stop! Do not let your mind go off on a journey to the Himalayas and put on ochre robes, get real. That is so nineteenth century! These days meditation is recognized as the top of the line multipurpose tool for working with anything that has to do with Human experience. The trick here is to find the right one for the right job because there are many different meditation techniques out there. Generally speaking though, they all work toward the development of mental discipline.

It is easier to focus our attention on activities that we are interested in and that we enjoy and we are easily distracted when doing things that we are not so interested in. And that distraction can easily mean the difference between success and failure. Also, who will have a better chance of higher levels of success, the person with a superficial understanding of a subject or the person who achieves a deeper insight through contemplation?

There is no question as to whether mental self discipline and success are linked together in a symbiotic relationship. The project manager who can grasp and focus on the relevant elements and determine priorities, and the homemaker who manages multiple tasks and activities in the daily events of family life are highly successful or barely competent depending on the level of self discipline they have developed which often translates into organized thinking skills. Self discipline is a key element of personal power, which can make the difference between being a victim of life and being the master of our lives.

Willpower is the ability to control yourself. Willpower is a certain level of inner strength. It can be associated with determination or even motivation. Willpower is what you use when you want to go out with friends but don't so that you can study. Willpower is what you use when you choose not to pick up a cigarette when you are trying to stop smoking. Willpower is how much power you have over yourself. Take a moment to reflect on what aspects of your life you maintain strong willpower in. Now, take a moment to reflect on aspects of your life in which you have limited willpower. Why do you think that is? What about this area of your life are you not as strong, determined, motivated or in control?

One of the tenets of personal development is to bring about a behavior change. If you want to develop yourself, you need to change your behavior to some degree. It is not necessarily overhauling yourself, but it's still a change.

The whole reason of self-improvement is to improve upon what you are. Some of things are not working for you, because the necessary behavior is absent. Or you just want to improve upon things. And you need new skills to achieve this improvement. Behavior change could also mean learning new skills.

When you learn new skill and actually apply new skills, the behavior change has taken place With this change, you exploit the benefits of the new skills.

So how does one change behavior? At the root of changing behavior is our capacity of self-discipline. This is also called self-control or willpower.

You can have all the knowledge in the world. But if you don't have the self-discipline to incorporate that knowledge in your behavior, the knowledge is of no use.

For example, you know that you are not supposed to do certain things. But if you do those things anyway, what is the point of the knowledge?

Personal development experts will tell you this: you have to set goals, divide tasks into sub tasks, prioritize tasks, write journals and have a positive attitude in spite of setbacks.

But if you don't have self-discipline to put all this advice into action, you won't succeed! And it may lead you to blame that expert advice doesn't work.

What is self-discipline though? It's the eternal conflict between the dual self. We always have a self who is conscious about long-term goals. He gets and remembers what is the right thing to do for us.

Then we have the other self which is impulsive and indulgent. This other self is always getting distracted towards the guilty pleasures that we should not explore. This other self is the one which blocks us from taking the initiative that we really should take.

The impulsive self is wanting a sweet treat, be lazy and just watch TV. While the better self is aware that those are bad things. And one should really be eating healthy in general, exercising and focusing on making that phone call and writing that journal.

At the deepest level, the impulsive self is a primitive self, who is impulsive, craving and desires things. The better self, is our analytical self. This is the neo-cortex in action. This is the recent part of our brain which engages in complex functions. This part of the brain has big picture, it weighs different options and knows what is right versus wrong.

Who doesn't want success, good relationships, health and well-being? Who doesn't want to be happy? And all of these can be achieved through proper self-discipline.

The fundamental reasons, most people don't succeed even after reading books, taking courses and attending seminars, is the failure to exercise self-discipline and giving into the impulsive self.

The root of all personal problems lies the failure of self-discipline. The fundamental reason people are not able to achieve success is because of them not able to keep up self-discipline.

Self-discipline is the biggest human strength.

You may wonder, if it's possible to increase self-discipline. And the answer is a resounding YES. One can definitely increase the levels of willpower he or she possesses.

Willpower is a limited resource. In other words self-discipline will deplete. Right after exercising self-discipline, your willpower will deplete and if you later have to exercise your willpower, you don't do that well.

Yet if you practice self-discipline over and over, it improves. This may sound counterintuitive. We just said that using willpower depletes it, but on the other hand we are saying that using it over and over, improves it. The best analogy to understand this is that of muscle. Right after use, muscle is fatigued and painful. But if you keep exercising repeatedly, your muscle strength and tone improves. If you intentionally practice self-discipline again and again, you'll build it up You will increase the level of self-discipline.

What are the ways to improve willpower?

Last decade of research in human psychology has revealed many ways in which one can improve the willpower or the self-discipline. A Stanford psychologist, Kelly McGonigal, identifies following four methods of improving the willpower.

Get enough sleep: One of the most common ways to improve willpower is through more sleep. Lack of sleep actually prevents us from operating at most willpower capacity. If we are sleep deprived, our prefrontal cortex doesn't activate enough, which means our restraining mind is not in action and we easily give in to the impulses.

It is important to get a good night's sleep. For most people 7 hours is what is required. If you haven't slept 7 hours and even if you don't feel sleepy, your cortex is still not working full capacity. Hence its very important to sleep 7 hours.

Meditation is one of the tools that can be effectively used to help with the increasing amount of sleep you can have.

Forgive yourself.

We are usually critical of ourselves. Especially when we have a setback, we tend to criticize us. Scientists found that for reasons we don't fully understand yet, when we criticize ourselves or when we are harsh on ourselves for setbacks, we tend to repeat such setbacks or the indulgent behavior.

On the other hand when you forgive yourself for the setbacks, it seems to have an effect of preventing future relapses. So learn to forgive yourself for setbacks along your journey.

Be mindful of distracting urge: One of the most important tool for boosting self-discipline is the awareness of your urges and impulses. If you can cultivate the mindful awareness of the distracting impulses, it becomes easier not to succumb. When you're struck with a distracting impulse or craving that will spoil your goal, you have to become mindful of that impulse.

We feel different types of impulses. You may feel like procrastinating and you won't start reading the book. Or you may feel like delaying that important class registration. If your goal is to lose weight, you may feel the impulse to indulge in high calorie food.

Here is what you do.

Notice the feeling that you're experiencing. Observe the thought that is going through your mind. Notice the impulse. Observe the itch.

Become aware of the impulse. Feel the impulse, what is it? What is the feeling? Where is the feeling? Is it in certain part of the body? Attend to this inner experience. Acknowledge the experience and then accept it. Don't try to run away from the experience. Face it head on and then accept it. Once accepted, take a deep breath and pause. Give your body a chance to slow down and plan. Once you have intimately observed the inner experience, bring your attention to your goal. Think of action that will help you achieve your goal.

This in essence is being mindful of your urge or impulse, then accepting it and moving on to what is the right thing to do.

This may be easier to do for food impulses. It is harder to be aware of your habit to put off things. But you can get better through practice.

Visualize the roadblocks.

Generally, people believe that you've to imagine success to become a success. Run of the mill self-help gurus will tell you that you've to imagine success to achieve success and not failure.

But exhaustive research proves that, just imagining the success is not enough. Yes imagining success is a good idea. But a better idea is to regularly imagine failure! You may think that will prime you for failure, but that's what doesn't happen in practice.

One scientific study compared two groups of people. One group just visualized the end goals. They visualized achieving the end goal.

Another group visualized the end goal along with the process of going through the journey to achieve success. The visualized ups and down of the process, they visualized the incremental improvement and progress that they were making along the journey.

The group that visualized the journey as well, was twice more likely to achieve the actual results.

So the journey towards achieving the goal is more important than the goal itself.

What is that you are going to inevitably face along the journey? Lots of setbacks. And for a faint heart, the setbacks will demoralize him and make him abandon his goal. There won't be just one setback, there will be plenty of them.

Failure is inevitable. And visualizing the failure prepares you for failure. After having repeatedly visualized failure along with the progress, when you're actually struck by the failure, it's no more a shock. You are already ready for it. So everyday visualize the journey and visualize a failure.

Make friends with your future self.

We don't normally think a lot about what would happen to us in future. We don't visualize our future self. Apparently our perception of our future self could be very influential when it comes to willpower.

If you think of future self as being totally different from your current self, in other words if you completely dissociate your current self from your future self, the future self becomes like a stranger and you wouldn't care much about future self.

In such cases, you don't bother to take care of future self as for all practical purposes future self is a stranger for you.

Different people have different perceptions about their future self. Some think of them more like their present self. Many think of their future self as very different.

The ability to disconnect from the long-term consequences of your choices primes you to be more impulsive. Even in the cases where choices are not relevant to future consequences.

In such cases, you become less attuned to your future concerns and plans. In reality we know that we need to take care of our future self. We need to save for retirement and we should take care of our future by taking care of our future self.

The key is how we can associate more with our future self? One interesting tool, researchers used effectively, is letter writing. Write a letter from your future self to your present self.

Or you can write to your current self, note down about who you are and what is going on in your life. Chronicle your current struggles. Then reply from your future self to current self.

The idea is to connect with your future self through correspondence. It is better to be optimistic in the letter that you write to future self than being completely pessimistic.

The purpose of this exercise is not to view this process as if you are fixing things for your future self. It is more about being able to feel that the future self is real and it is going to be you. It's not so much that it's going to be same person that you are now.

Even if you start imagining doing mundane stuff in the future. Like driving to work, or going to shop or talking with friends or doing chores in the household. Imagine vividly what it's going to feel like many years down the line.

Take personal responsibility.

By placing ownership for things we are not coming through on, off on something or someone else, we give the control over our decisions where it should not be going. Willpower requires control of yourself, if you are handing it over to another person or thing, you will never have enough willpower to change or complete what you are trying to do. Begin increasing willpower by taking full responsibility for decisions and actions that you take. In return you will see both your willpower and discipline rise.

Watch your Self Talk

By watching how you talk to yourself as you make decisions you are reinforcing your personal responsibility and freedom as a person. But just as important, the way you talk to yourself has an influence over your confidence and inner strength. When you lack confidence and inner strength, you will notice that your willpower goes down. If you are consistently talking down to yourself, you decrease the level of key factors that can boost your willpower. The stronger you feel about yourself, the more inner strength you will have to make decisions that are in your best interest. Increase willpower by talking kindly to yourself.

Define your Purpose

In business, you have to have a 3 and 5 year plan. Why? Because it gives you and those around you a direction and a vision. You must have a purpose in each choice that you make for your company so that it moves in the direction of your goals. You need this same plan in life. Create weekly, monthly and yearly goals or plans for yourself, and put them in a place where you can see these goals each day. Then, each time you make a choice, be sure that it is in line with your purpose and direction. If you know why you are here in this world and if you understand where you desire to go, then your willpower and control over your choices will be stronger. Take time to reflect on your purpose in life. Create goals and plans for your future and take these into account with each decision you make.

Avoid Willpower Depletion

Depletion of willpower can lead to stress which inactivates the prefrontal cortex and this can result in uncontrollable mood swing as well as indulgences, followed by a feeling of defeat which can make you to fall back on harmful old habits. It is very vital to flex your willpower muscle in order to keep it in shape but you should also give it a break. Hence, there is the need to strike a balance between the two so as to avoid unnecessary depletion. It is also important for you to avoid taking too much at once. For example, do not try to stop drinking coffee, break your nail-biting habit, stop smoking and start a new fitness plan, all at the same time. You should take them one after the other.

Master The Art of Building Good Habits. Having good habits is very vital for building your willpower because when you are stressed up, you are more likely to fall back to your old habits. For example, some people fall back to alcohol after a stressful day but if you develop a good habit after a stressful day, like going for a 10-minute walk, your body will no longer crave for alcohol but the walk.

THE POWER OF SELF-DISCIPLINE

Self-discipline is a powerful, potent and priceless trait of successful people. It's a quality people admire and secretly wish they possessed. Your ability to develop self-discipline will contribute more to your success than any other quality, trait or habit. Your good looks, great personality and passion will carry you only so far. But self-discipline will take you across the finish line.

Self-discipline is the ability to take action in a situation, regardless of your emotional state. When you are self-disciplined, you decide what actions to take today to get the results you desire. You do what you need to do, whether you want to do it or not. Self-discipline helps you keep the promises and commitments you make to yourself and clients. You do what you commit to and see it through to the end. No excuses!

Many people in sales and business often say, "I'm just not disciplined;" "I was never one to see things through to the end;" or "I get started, but then something happens, and I get off track." Those are the words of business owners who would rather make excuses than be disciplined and take action. Every time you make excuses, you choose to stay stuck in a never ending loop of famine and drought in your business. The moment your feet hit the floor in the morning you have a choice. Will I make excuses or will I make money today? The choice is yours.

Do you cringe at the idea of repeating an activity that you find difficult or doing a task over and over again in order to perfect it? Developing a skill that doesn't come naturally to you can feel like a daunting task. You start the process but, inevitably, never see it through to completion because of a lack of self-discipline. The task may have become too difficult to persevere, so you give up. When you lack self-discipline, it's easier to give up than to push through to the other side.

Discipline drives your actions, attitudes, behaviors and outcomes. When you lack discipline and don't have a clear understanding of what you want, why you want it and how to get it, you will be met with a series of setbacks and disappointments. Your life will be filled with frustration, anxiety and failure. It doesn't have to be that way.

Self-discipline is required to complete difficult, tedious, or unpleasant tasks and activities. Tasks and activities that require the most self-discipline are also the most rewarding, yield bigger results and have higher payoffs.

Never underestimate the power of self-discipline. It's the foundation needed to succeed in any endeavor and is essential for increasing sales and growing your business. There's no area in your life where self-discipline has greater impact on your future than in your business.

How is it that some people consistently manifest and turn their dreams and ideas into actions and achievements, while others dream, think, and plan, but accomplish very little? Self-discipline! There is a huge difference between thinking and doing. Dreaming and thinking lead you nowhere. Doing the work and taking action leads to results. Self-discipline is for everyone. You, too, can learn and develop this hot commodity, but once you develop self-discipline, you must practice it constantly.

Albert Gray says, "The common denominator of success-the secret of success of every man who has ever been successful-lies in the fact that he formed the habit of doing things that failures don't like to do."

Stepping-up and taking responsibility for the quality of your life and the success of your business are scary and intimidating. You have to muster your inner strength and be disciplined to get things done. It's like trading in your security blanket for a parachute.

Achieving sales success is the result of a foundation grounded in right attitudes, mixed with positive self-esteem and unshakable self-discipline. You can possess all the right skills and have a great product or service, but if you lack the right attitude, sooner or later, lack of self-control or discipline will sabotage your sales results.

If you want to be as successful entrepreneur and millionaire you must develop this habit of self-discipline because it is without doubt the single most important characteristic that you will ensure your success in all areas of your life.

There is no point in setting long-term or short-term goals if you're not going to have the self-control and self-discipline to tenaciously do what is required of you to bring them to fruition. If you have high self-discipline you will eventually achieve your long-term goals in all areas of your life.

Look around you at the failures in life and notice the difference between those are high levels of discipline and those who have very little or no discipline. People that fail simply do what losers do and the winners follow through and do what has to be done. Losers are not prepared to pay the price, even if they know what they are supposed to do, they still do not do it. Why? Because they simply do not have sufficient self-discipline to follow through on their commitments, to themselves and others.

Millionaires realises that they need to pay a price for success and consequently get into the habit of mastering themselves, directing themselves, and concerning themselves with achieving results. They do what it takes and don't allow tension relieving behaviour to take charge of them.

That does not mean that if you exercise high self-discipline that you have to sacrifice every pleasure in your life. You must just learn to play hard and work hard and to exercise good judgement in setting your priorities.

If you learn to have self-discipline you will find that your self-esteem and confidence also improves because you have more control on your business activities and private life.

One way to increasing your self-discipline is to have a fanatical focus on the goals you want to achieve and what you must do to achieve them. Identify those areas of your life which are stagnating due to inactivity and make a commitment today to develop self-discipline in those areas. Habits are developed by repeating a desired action or behaviour on a regular basis until it becomes embedded in your behavioural profile.

In the beginning, it may take a lot of willpower to do what you have to do. But remember that self-discipline becomes easier the more exercises it.

You have the power to control your thoughts and direct them to do your bidding. Make an effort to improve your self-discipline by controlling yourself in the same way that you would suddenly change your behaviour if, while you were having a heated argument with a member of the family, the doorbell rang. You would then instantly be able to control yourself to save yourself embarrassment and simply because you desired to do so. Deliberately think the sort of thoughts that you desire and you will become a person of self-control.

Avoid procrastination at all costs and never delay until tomorrow what you can do today. It is a tremendous waste of energy and can lead to failure.

One sure way to develop self-discipline is to associate with those people who are self-disciplined and exhibit higher self-control. Like attracts like, surround yourself with the right kind of people and their positive attributes will be infectious.

Self Discipline, the Number One Key to Success

If you seriously want to master and dominate every aspect of your life, then it is very expedient that you develop the virtue of self discipline. It is very inevitable if you want to have substantial achievement and reach your heart desires. Setting goals and targets are not enough to be successful in any endeavour. You need to work persistently on them and for that to be possible to a large extent, self discipline is highly needed. I am yet to see anyone who has made outstanding achievement and success without discipline. It is the number one attribute one must possess to attain excellence in business, sports, personal development etc.

One who is self disciplined finds it easy to make decision, whether big or small. They take action quickly based on the decision made. Even in spite of challenges, and discomfort, they still persist until their goal is achieved. Based on what have been discussed so far, what then is self discipline? It is simply the ability to refrain from instant gratification and force yourself to do thing that you should do whether you like it or not, in comfort or not. You have to give up short term pleasures in order to achieve a worthwhile goal.

To be disciplined means that you stick to plans and action that leads to the realization of your goal. It also means having self control which eventually leads to self mastery. To fully develop the habit of self discipline, one has to be consistent in taking disciplined actions daily.

To be disciplined does not connote living a reclusive, constricted or narrow-minded life. It does not also mean that you should give up pleasures, enjoyment at all times. Self discipline gives you the ability to focus your attention on your aims and objectives until they are attained. It means blocking away any form of distraction that may want to arise to take you away from what you hope to achieve. Self discipline gives order to life.

Ways To Have and Increase Your Willpower

Have a strong desire to achieve a particular goal as self-discipline needs inspiration and motivation. Remember that every great victory requires great sacrifice. Therefore, make sacrifices in the form of time, effort, and hard work.

Find mentors or role models that push you upward. And keep yourself accountable to bring the best results.

Have a plan to get there, and get a clear vision of what you want and a clear deadline in place. Be consistent with it and repeat day in and day out.

Discipline yourself to follow your actions through until the end.

Build the habit of choosing what is hard and necessary over what is fun and easy to do.

Take actions to make your goals reality because life changes only to the extent that you change.

Cultivate qualities such as patience, persistence, enthusiasm, tenacity, courage, optimism and passion for nourishing your willpower.

Visualize your desired outcomes. Act as if you were already successful.

Keep going if you encounter failure and adversity. Face the challenges in life and endure them long enough to succeed. No one else is going to climb the ladder of success for you.

Create small milestones to increase your willpower and move forward by making decisions that contribute to your objectives.

Self-discipline is committing to do whatever it takes, no matter the challenges and how hard it may be.

Use other's experience to better discipline yourself along your journey.

Get inspired and enjoy the process to maintain a high level of self-discipline.

Do not blame, complain or use excuses.

There are several ways of developing self-discipline, but the best and effective way is by deliberately refusing to attend to desires and pleasure that are not important. Endless temptations and desires that are of no significant importance confronts everyone daily, but by practicing to ignore them, you get stronger. In my next article, I will discuss some of the methods of developing self discipline.

Some Benefits Of Self discipline

Your confidence level increases. -By developing the habit of discipline consistently, you level of self esteem increases which eventually increase your level of confidence.

You will become more productive and accomplish more in less time. When you refuse to pay attention to temptations and desires that tend to distract you and limit your pace of work, your level of productivity increases. You will achieve far more in less time.

Ability to stay calm and positive in the midst of challenges and obstacles. Challenges and obstacle are bound to arise when planning to achieve your goals. It takes the habit of self discipline to stay on course no matter the circumstances.

Life becomes easy and cheap when you are disciplined.

Better Finance, good health, happy relationship with others etc. The benefits of living a disciplined life are endless. It is never too late to set goals and resolve to be discipline to attain them. Project your life into the future and visualize what you desire to attain or become. Have it in mind that you will only achieve what you see when you are discipline. When you have a picture of your projected goal in mind, you will find it easily to delay instant gratification and pleasure because in the long run, they will lead you away from you heart desires.

CHAPTER 3

The Ultimate Guide To Learn How To Develop Powerful Daily Habits To Program Your Mind, Build Mental Strength, Self-Confidence And Grit

Self-confidence plays such an important role in our life on a daily basis. Most of the time we just go on with your day without ever thinking about how confident we feel about ourselves - that is, until we're faced with a huge decision or we need to perform a certain task and expect to do it well.

So creating a solid mindset to feel completely confident anytime and anywhere becomes a very important quality that we can apply to most situations before they ever occur, thus making those challenging moments so much easier to contend with and to help us feel better about them.

For most of us, trying just one method to gain confidence and maintain a confident mindset doesn't always prove to be the best solution, but using a combination of several techniques may provide exactly the key outcome to successfully achieve our ultimate goal.

Here are 10 strategies to the solutions that can be used alone, or in a combination to create or change your mindset to gain the self confidence you deserve. (not necessarily in order of importance).

1. One of the first and most important concepts to the creation of a strong and sound mindset is to begin with a clear slate. In other words, to erase those obstacles from your past that continue to form negative beliefs which keep you from feeling confident. It's pretty difficult to move forward if you are constantly haunted by negative experiences from your past.

You can start the healing process by writing down all those past influences that continue to make you feel inadequate, indecisive, and insecure. I like to refer to this as clearing your mindset closet. Once you've discharged these destructive experiences, you can begin to create new positive associations that will propel you to new horizons.

2. Another destructive behavior is to focus on negative situations and outcomes. If you tell yourself that bad things always happen to you, then your subconscious mind will continue to find ways to reinforce that and constantly remind your thought process that "this is just the way it has been and there is nothing you can do about it".

So this destructive thought pattern becomes the norm and you'll have a very difficult time getting away from this type of behavior (in my book, The 51st State, I refer to this as 'stinkin-thinkin'). Of course, not everything is going to produce a positive result for you, but you can DECIDE that negative outcomes are merely lessons to which you should view as a sign to try a new approach.

Don't let your mind say to you; "see, I told you only bad things happen" - keep thinking that way and most likely, they will.

3. So, with a clear head and a positive attitude, you can begin to create your positive belief programming by some very powerful and influential techniques to disrupt a negative situation that occurs anytime, anywhere.

Be prepared to change your environment, or enhance the mood, or by documenting the cause so you can avoid a similar outcome in the future. You can put on some loud and fun music, you can go for a walk or run to exert some energy, you can listen to inspiring messages (i.e. my audio session) to help empower mindset and deal with a situation better, or take a hot bath to relax you physically.

Decide for yourself, what works for you to quickly change the immediate circumstances and you will open new channels to overcome these challenges.

4. Create a vision (dream) board that you can look at constantly. This is a great way to form positive beliefs and give you a physical "goal getter" to refer to first thing in the morning, last thing in the evening, and anytime in between.

You can use a bulletin board, white board, electronic graphic on your computer, or a simple cardboard poster that you can attach pictures, quotes, and goals as a constant reminder of what you want, who you want to be, and how you want to feel. Just remember to use this inspiration as often as possible.

Look at it, read it, study it, dream it, and believe in it. You can gain some huge confidence in yourself when you create some visual goals.

5. Surround yourself with positive energy. As obvious as this sounds, I'm amazed how many people continue to let destructive influences into their life from others. Join a group of like-minded people that you can relate to and share with and that empower you, or start one.

Stop hanging around those individuals that suck your energy from you and bring you down. Start associating with those you lift you up and energize you and you will probably find yourself with more confidence.

There is so much great opportunity to build confidence when you truly relate to others who recognize your strengths and talents instead of those who want to steal your dreams. Think back on those pivotal moments when someone you met made a huge impact on your life (in a positive way of course) and realize that this can, and probably will happen again.

Set your own boundaries and limits about who you will let become part of your circle of influence and you can feel the incredible power of confidence.

6. Getting busy with physical exercise (only with doctor's permission) is probably one the most empowering methods to build self confidence. I have heard from so many people that this is the one thing that really makes them feel incredibly confident physically, mentally, and emotionally.

Sure, you may seek to build muscle, lose a few pounds, look fit, but it's the mental aspect that has a huge impact on building confidence.

Just knowing that it takes motivation and perseverance to get out and exercise is very satisfying by itself. Stick with it for awhile, and you should realize some really great physical results from your efforts. It's also a great stress reliever and tension reducer.

There are many ways to get active, from going to the gym, to walking around the block, to working out at home with simple weights or a cardio DVD. You don't have to set huge milestones to shoot for and accomplish at first. Start out with small, achievable goals in the beginning and continue to increase your workout program until you reach your ultimate results. Find something that you can do physically on a regular basis and you can gain the confidence you desire from this terrific form of activity.

7. Accomplish something, no matter how insignificant it seems, that gives you some satisfaction that you are moving in the right direction. Confidence comes from results - usually positive results.

Don't just sit around and wait for things to come your way. Get up and call someone, or open a business account, write a blog post, clean the closet, even plant a garden, something that is necessary to help you move forward.

There certainly are no guarantees that is will provide instant success for you, but it keeps the motivation factor progressing and hopefully will lead you to the next task to accomplish to reach your goals (you better have some goals).

8. Develop some mind-healthy habits of positive reinforcement. Most of us have read motivational quotes to some degree. They can be found all over our busy world, from television commercials, to inspirational wall hangings, to fortune cookie messages, to seminars and programs you can listen to anywhere you go. That's terrific.

There is such a vast amount of really great messages to keep us inspired all the time. Now, we just have to channel them into our subconscious mind so we create (or change) our belief system. Just reading a great quote or hearing a positive message usually isn't enough to really embed that positive idea firmly in our mind so that we can call on it when we need to.

Try affirmations, mantras, and meditation, that can have a lasting result and provide a positive memory bank that we can tap into at will. A more consistent approach is usually required to create this part of NLP (neuro-linguistic programming). Put these words of confidence anywhere you spend a lot of time at or on a regular basis.

By reading these powerful messages constantly, you can begin to create your own beliefs that will flush away negative thoughts and replace them with empowering and confident ones.

9. Be grateful, thankful, and appreciative of the gifts you already possess. You may be asking; how is this going to give me more confidence? The solution is that we can take a step back and realize who we already are, what we've already accomplished, and what we already have in our lives.

We all have certain gifts that we should be so thankful for. Sometimes it's hard to think about them when we are struggling with life's challenges. This is a great time to make a list of our wonderful traits and characteristics and pin them up on our dream board so that we can refer to them when life becomes difficult.

Confidence in our ability to appreciate the things we have instead of constantly striving for more can have a profound effect on our mindset. That also leads to rethinking what we really want and who we really want to be. Take some time to write down your gifts and be confident with them.

10. Never, ever give up. That means never give up on your dreams, your beliefs, or your talents. There is a time when you may be smart to let go of something that is draining you mentally, physically, emotionally, and financially so you can move on to more progressive tasks that will propel you forward in seeking your ultimate success.

You can usually decide when this time is appropriate when it just feels right to part from something that stops you in your tracks or takes too much away from you. It may be a relationship, a j.o.b., a business venture or a destructive circle of influences.

You should be focused on that which gets you closer to success by helping you accomplish your tasks and reach your goals. Sure there will be unexpected challenges along the way, but don't let them bring you down and away from your dreams. You can just expect that challenges will happen, but you can also prepare for some of them by thinking ahead to what is presented in front of you.

Prioritize your tasks, contact those you need help from, and always take some action to get you closer to individual goals.

Try applying as many of these methods to increase your confidence and you may experience a higher power never felt before. Your mindset is so important to your confidence levels, which in turn helps you make decisions, take action, and venture out of your comfort zone, that can lead to the road to realize your ultimate success.

Focus on making things happen that move you forward and stop wasting time on things that are nonproductive. Confidence crushers are found too easily and in so many aspects of life so weeding through them can prove to turn confidence levels positive by eliminating those things that are destructive.

Re-program your subconscious mind

The subconscious mind is something most of us are aware of, but do you realise the power of your subconscious mind, we really do take it for granted! Learn how to make it work for you instead of seemingly against you?

So what exactly is the subconscious mind? Well this is the part of the mind where we store all of our memories both good and bad. Think of it as a computer, how much stuff have you downloaded and saved but forgotten you have it? Tons right, yeah well it is the same in your subconscious mind, every single moment you experience is stored in your memory bank, and you may think it has gone but..oh no, it is still there buried amongst the cobwebs. Now here is one for you to ponder on; if you believe that you have lived before and maybe even had many lives, do you think it is possible that your subconscious mind has stored those memories? Something to think about eh?

Anything we do on auto pilot is done by the subconscious, like driving our car everyday, we don't need to think about it, we learnt it and stored the knowledge in our memory. So if we learn bad habits then, this is also stored right?

So what is stored in your memory, what sort of childhood did you have? Now hopefully you had a beautiful childhood with a loving family who said positive things and encouraged your dreams, these memories are stored and you will continue for the rest of your life to create loving people who you trust totally all around you, because your subconscious mind knows nothing else, unless that is, that you learn a different lesson along the way!

Any trauma or event that caused fear in us is stored right there in our memory bank, this is how we create phobias, and how we repeat the same old annoying patterns that do not serve our growth, and even worse send us reeling backwards and doubting what we previously learned from good experience. Most of the time we don't even realise that we are repeating patterns, I think most of us have heard the words " why do you keep doing this? When are you going to stop making the same mistakes?"

You see if we experience something negative, the subconscious mind will create the memory in a fashion that will allow us to cope with it, and if we are not strong at the time or the trauma is particular bad, it could possibly block the memory completely to keep us safe, but the memory does not go away, for instance if you had a bad experience as a five year old, and then if a similar experience shows up in your adult life you will react just like your five year old did, and you will be left confused, not recognising your self and wondering why the heck you reacted the way you did. So if for instance you were abandoned by some one you loved as a child and then someone in your adult life leaves you,

you will either kick and scream or do nothing to save it, just put it away and cease to feel. Scary stuff I know, so what can we do about it? (this is a block and needs to be dealt with and removed)

Well you will be happy to know that there is tons you can do about it! This is your life, your body and your mind! You have the power to re-program your subconscious mind and make it work for you, it is your friend just trying to keep you safe and you need to get to know it, accept it and acknowledge it, tune and refine it so that it creates good patterns for your life and keeps you on a perfect track to your choices for happiness and harmony, yes it really is in your power! The subconscious mind is a fascinating subject with no limits, use it to create the life you want.

Why Re-Program the Subconscious?

In consideration and appreciation of this vast, influential, and powerful component of our mind, most of us would prefer a life that continuously expands in a positive way, benefiting us individually and as a natural by-product, the well being of others. Once realizing this noble desire in a practical sense, the implications for enhancing all of life will eventually be profound, as we will become less unconsciously relational to one another.

By connecting the two minds cohesively in a meaningful way and acknowledging their interactions, we can begin the process to re-program portions of our subconscious mind that are responsible for self-sabotaging our best, highest intentions and desires. In the normal, daily course of life we occasionally encounter repetitive yet seemingly hidden symptoms stored in our subconscious that hinder experiencing our highest purpose usually displayed as more joy, productivity, success and balanced living. It is at this point when awareness arises and we begin to recognize something is affecting our actions and with the best intentions determine to resolve these conflicts within us.

This is the turning point filled with great opportunity! The best examples of these deeply hidden symptoms generated by the subconscious are those having a "memory signature" of significant emotional power. One such stored example is feeling rejection from someone you care for or love. At the next situation involving a perceived potential for rejection, our conscious mind will quickly receive an embedded conclusion from the subconscious to justify why rejection will happen. Even though this is a false assumption, you may unknowingly be the one rejecting in advance, any possibility to experience full acceptance that another person or situation may offer. The same goes for high, emotionally charged low self-esteem conflicts that where created every time you experienced the feelings of inadequacy, assumed failure or when someone implied or called you ignorant, worthless, lazy or worse!

All these negative connotations exude very powerful imagery that unless countered or removed entirely from your subconscious makeup, will lead to a lifelong cycle of struggle in many areas of your life. Reprogramming your subconscious to counteract the negatively charged embedded responses is not that difficult if you are willing to apply a few simple procedures that over time, will greatly improve your mental balance and outward response to life as a whole.

The How To

Fortunately for those who wish to venture into changing themselves for the better, a few established approaches are available to successfully re-program your subconscious mind. These methods overwrite unwanted responses by replacing them with a different or more positive oriented influences within the mental construct deep in the mind.

Your subconscious programming did not evolve overnight- it was solidified and strengthened each time a matching response was warranted and offered up in response to a conscious thought created in waking life. In consideration of this fact, a fundamental key to remember is these methods exponentially become more effective and produce rapid results through their consistent application. Below are five effective (and advanced) methods to begin the reprogramming process.

Visualization

The subconscious responds very well to visual stimuli. Viewing images that create pleasing and emotionally uplifting thoughts of appreciation, joy, and gratitude will plant positive imagery within the subconscious exactly as if you physically experienced them. The subconscious cannot differentiate real from the imaginary being as it is influenced by emotions only. Collect together pleasing imagery from any sources that you view to induce positive feelings. Repetition of viewing these images provide for an eventuality whereby the physical images are not necessary and at will, can be recalled anywhere anytime within the mind's eye.

Affirmations

There is no simpler way to inject positive messages into the subconscious. Create simple statements crafted in the present tense NOT future sense. For example- "I am" rather than "I will". There is no future sense only the present moment for the subconscious. This is a very important distinction. Match the words with corresponding feelings and images associated with the affirmative statement. Repetitive replay is the key to success using well-crafted affirmations so you can verbally or internally express them anytime, anywhere. These are very powerful when done correctly.

Environmental Influence

Some say we are a reflection of the company or environment we keep. It's true- everyone lives the reality they expect. External interactions with people, places, or events have the potential to exert mental impressions into the subconscious mind equally positive or negative. Your best guidance is to balance with the conscious mind and heart, an appropriate emotional response given the external influence regardless of the initial emotional response you feel. For example, when confronted with potentially unwanted experiences, filter your response by seeking out something about the event that is positive. Remain focused on any positive aspects to neutralize a negative response or unwanted influence from being placed into the subconscious.

Hypnosis

Here is a scientifically proven method which has withstood the test of time, and within a proper setting has immense potential to offer help. Under a trained practitioner, hypnosis can jumpstart subconscious reprogramming by effectively bypassing the conscious, filtering portion of our mind. This time saving, short-cut method is very effective for many since it quickly alters behavior through implantation of specific modification or belief statements into the subconscious. Typically one seeks out a well qualified expert in the field of hypnosis to facilitate personalized sessions to effect results.

Brain Entrainment

Another very popular method with similar effects to hypnosis without the need of a hypnotist is entrainment of the mind. Think-self-hypnosis. Modern science has revealed unique, variable frequencies our minds exhibit while in various mental states. If one were to induce via virtually inaudible influential statements or positive affirmations while you are in one of these specific brain frequencies states such as those present while in deep meditation, alterations to the subconscious can be quickly realized. Again, repetition of use is very important while employing this method. Many good sources of brain entrainment audios are widely available with most designed to target a focused, specific change within the subconscious. Equally important, some entrainment audios are well designed in that they are co-mingled with pleasing soundtracks.

Reprogramming Checkup List

Here are 17 points of light to remember, contemplate and apply habitually while inducing desired changes to your subconscious. Really, this is a lifestyle and noble undertaking which produces rich rewards both personally and in the greater world around you. So, below are some well know and lesser known, easily applied thoughts and actions to help you along facilitating a new, improved you! Find what resonates with you and notice what those feeling are (no matter positive or negative) when reviewing the list. This feeling-based response will provide you with valuable emotionally directed insights of those items which will improve your life the quickest when applied. Your higher-self is always your best guidance. That still, small voice never misleads you. Acknowledge this higher, unbiased guidance and reap phenomenal improvements in all areas of your life. Like they say- It's good to take a checkup from the neck up regularly.

First and foremost, believe in yourself.

Understand what is holding you back so you can overcome it.

Spend time in quiet self-reflection, prayer, or meditation at least once a day.

Guard all that comes into your mind and all that leaves your mind.

Know what you want in very specific terms.

Remove all sources of negativity from your life.

Surround yourself with positive, success-minded people.

Create a realistic plan to attain your deepest desires.

Take positive steps each day toward what you want to attract.

Focus on the present - as if you have already attracted the things you want.

Create visual reminders of your goals and intentions.

Make a recording of your favorite affirmations or buy a self-hypnosis CD.

Avoid conflicting messages by matching your feelings with your desires.

Write a newspaper report about your success as if it has already happened.

Be an advocate for yourself, allowing praise and compliments.

Choose to carry a positive attitude at all times. œ Have an attitude of gratitude.

The Conscious Mind's Role

The conscious mind has a valuable role in reshaping our sometimes-illusive subconscious mind. One of the best and note-worthy attributes of an awakened state is that of becoming aware of both our own thoughts and reactions to daily life with all its apparent distractions. We could easily imagine the conscious portion of our mind as the proverbial gatekeeper.

While as simplistic as this may seem, really for those of us who desire more joy in life, simplicity has great value and is not to be discarded in this valiant endeavor. Utilize and enlist the help of the left, analytical portion of your brain while at the same time, not ignoring the right brain's intuitive influence. By doing so, you have a powerful, to-the-point vigilant ally readily available to monitor and assist as you progress along.

Allow the conscious mind's gentle reminders of your thoughts and responses even actions you take among daily activities. By deliberately fine tuning your thoughts as the happen, is an important key that ultimately delivers the type of results you are looking for. Through just a few practical, conscious applications of what you have learned here will in very little time, become second nature and open doors of higher-consciousness that flood the subconscious with a more positive, redirection of thoughts. In short order, actual improvements and related changes will be visually observable to both you and those around you.

Set Action Steps And Definitive Goals

In order for anyone to have a level of success in life, it is necessary to create a goal to aim for. What you choose for a goal will begin to attract ideas and resources towards you that will help you accomplish those goals. The first place to begin is to write down as many goals as you can think of right now on a piece of paper.

As you are writing those ideas down, what you desire will begin to appear. You must ensure that each goal you write down follows these guidelines:

1) Must be personal to you;

2) Must be achievable;

3) Your goals must be realistic.

I point those specific guidelines out to you because far too many people write that they have a goal to make a million dollars, when realistically they are just barely able to make $500.00/week. A goal should be something you will achieve or want in the next 6 months.

By following the guidelines above, spend an hour or so writing down as many goals as you want to achieve in the next six months. This will give you a target that we will be able to work with. Once you have your goals written out, we will begin the next step.

Having goals can be exciting, but for some people the idea of having a goal can be intimidating. Questions begin to form inside their mind with thoughts around failure. Some people never fulfill their personal desires, because of a fear of failure. There are numerous articles that are written to help assist with the fear of failure and other negative thought patterns.

Once you have your ten goals written down, the next step is to determine which of those goals would give you the most positive change if you were to accomplish it immediately. By doing this exercise, you will be able to identify your major definitive purpose.

The goal that we want to focus on during the next six months is the one you just identified as your major definitive purpose. Write your goal down on a 3 inch by 5 inch card and review it at least 3 times a day, morning, noon and night. Ask yourself, "How will I accomplish this goal." Each time you ask write down the thoughts that you get on the card.

The idea of continually asking yourself "How" will begin to activate your subconscious mind and you will receive the answers you desire.

The final step is to take action. Do not let 24 hours pass without completing at least one thing on your list, every 24 hours. Keep up with writing new ideas and crossing off completed ideas, and before you know it, you will have reached your goal.

CHAPTER 4

MANAGE AND UTILIZE YOUR EMOTIONS

Managing emotions is an arduous task for some but a skill that is essential to success in business and personal relationships. We all have and experience emotions whether we like it or not. Managing emotions mainly deals with unpleasant emotions: anger, fear, frustration, depression, despair. Emotions are the feelings we experience day to day, such as happiness, pride, boredom, sadness, anger and frustration. Emotions are a part of our everyday existence as they move through the body, affecting our state-of-mind, performance, health and energy. Emotions cannot be helped. Emotions we don't even realize we are feeling can influence our thoughts and behaviors; they can also travel from person to person like a virus. Due to this virus like state, it is of the most upmost importance for those in positions of influence not only their own emotions but understand the need to monitor and perhaps influence the moods of others.

Management is in a unique position to dictate the pulse and rhythm in their workplace. "We engage in emotional contagion," says Sigal Barsade, a Wharton management professor who studies the influence of emotions on the workplace. Broken promises, laying the blame on others, dishonest communications, and ignoring employee suggestions are all unfortunately very commonplace in real world management. So how does management expect their employees to manage their emotions in the workplace if the tone that is being set is negative or one of disregard? Without that emotional-management component, a work environment can become toxic.

Those in leadership positions are often not really good at working with people and so spend a lot of their time avoiding and/or strategizing how to deal with, avoid, or get rid of those who are troubling. In fact a great deal of leadership is actually about emotion management. Emotions are also essential to inspirational leadership. These managers often lack the necessary people skills, communication skills and leadership skills to influence the emotional tone of the workplace. This is a critical oversight by those in upper management who do not get or provide the training to create a positive emotional tone. So in turn, employees' moods, emotions, and overall dispositions impact job performance, decision making, creativity, turnover, teamwork, negotiations and leadership.

For Management to be in complete control of emotions of the workplace, they need to be a master of themselves, both theirs and their employees'. It is essential for employees to positive at work—but this has to be supported by upper management. Employees need positive feedback, and if they do not see that coming, or do not even get acknowledged for their work, they will look elsewhere. This creates turnover and increased costs and lowered performance. Many employers in the current economy are quick to just higher someone else rather than address this aspect. They fail to look at the long term costs of losing an employee in downtime and in the retraining of a new employee.

One of the most fundamental things necessary to improve employees' attitude and to create a "culture of love," is to adopt systems that recognize and reward those positive attitudes and behaviors. When managers are manipulative and treat employees just as "equipment" rather than humans beings, poor attitudes follow. And a workplace where emotions run rampant can turn off employees, vendors and customers alike. Similarly, it is the duty of the manager to ensure that he manages the negative emotional attitudes of his team in such a way that such attitudes are not reflected in their performance. Managers also need to learn how to lead by the example they set -how to deal with their own pain in positive ways that can inspire others to deal differently with their own difficult situations. Barsade gave the example of a manager who was dragged down at the start of every day when passing by the desk of an employee who either grunted or gave no acknowledgement. The manager took control and simply started following a different route through the office. If the company is losing money and experiencing the effects of downsizing, should the manager, feeling stressed and overwhelmed, convey his despair to his workers. Or should the manager try to appear cheerful and act as if nothing is wrong. Barsade says it's possible for the manager to convey emotions that are both authentic and positive, saying something like, "I know you're worried. The ability to summon positive emotions during trying times of stress is the key to being a successful manager.

Most organizations have traditionally focused on teaching logical and rational thinking and have neglected emotional learning in their development programs. The main implication is that organizations should focus on hiring managers with high emotional and social competence and also provide EI training and development opportunities to managers to enable them create a positive organizational climate. Effective listening is an important aspect of learning to do that as well.

Listening effectively is difficult because people vary in their communication skills and in how clearly they express themselves, and often has different needs, wants and purposes for interacting. Still, listening is an important skill and needs to be taught. The most basic of all human needs is the need to understand and to be understood. Feedback must take into account the needs of both the giver and the receiver. Otherwise, it can be destructive when it fails to consider the needs and feelings of everyone involved. Listen to words, body language and emotions to understand the player's both conscious and unconscious needs. By feeling heard, many negative consequences of a disgruntled or upset employee can be lowered if not stopped all together.

Managing emotions does not mean denying their existence or ignoring them. Never tell an employee he should not feel that way.

Feelings are a biological reaction a circumstance, event or stressor and cannot be helped. How one can help is to acknowledge the feelings and help the employee consider positive possible choices they have to resolve their current feelings. Take a minute to consider the importance of active listening by thinking about how you can be a good active listener in terms of body language—or what you do during communication, voice—how you respond to the speaker, and content—what you say when you respond to the speaker. Active listening is an effective tool to reduce the emotionality of a situation. Every manager or sales team leader that can learn these skills will find that their team will overall increase in company loyalty and performance. Managing emotions is something that must be addressed, not avoided for success.

The brain is more then a complex organ in the human body, it is a tool that can be polished to work better. The part of the brain where emotions reside is the Deep Limbic Center, which is located near the center of the brain, while the part of the brain that controls emotional impulses is the Frontal Lobe located within the Neocortex which is the part of the brain that caused human beings as a race to evolve beyond the Neanderthal mentality. You can regard your brain as more then an organ or even a tool. Think of it as a muscle that can be strengthened and such strength begins with the development and growth of your emotional intelligence.

Emotional intelligence or EI for short is defined as the way one understands controls and evaluates their emotions. There are four branches of EI which are:

• Perceiving Emotions: One of the first branches in understanding emotion is how we perceive them which may involve understanding body language and facial expressions

• Reasoning with Emotions: The second branch which involves using one's emotions to better promote cognitive activity as our emotions decide what we are most interested in.

- Understanding Emotions: The third branch which involves the way that you understand and perceive other's emotions.
- Managing Emotions: The forth and final branch which is the vital key to the strengthening of emotional intelligence and the way that we respond to certain things.

The process of emotional intelligence can be very beneficial to people who seek to improve themselves and strengthen their personal development. If you can control the way your emotions are managed and perceived then you can in turn utilize the full power of your mind.

EI works sort of like positive affirmation, the power of your own thoughts and processes within your brain can bring favorable results and improvement in your personal growth. For example if you master the management of your own emotions then you will not be prone to bad emotional impulse control and will be calmer, more collected and better able to process and absorb information which will lead to a more powerful mind.

The development of EI could also change the way that your Deep Limbic System works as it is the place not only where emotions are stored but also where you develop your unconscious values and better self awareness may even change some of those values as well in a good way that promotes less hostility, judgment and ignorance. You in turn will not only have a stronger brain but will also be a much better you.

If the idea of mastering your own emotions in favor of a stronger mind appeals to you then emotional intelligence may be instrumental in the achievement of that as well as a smarter, more intuitive, more self-controlled you that can change your life in a variety of positive and long lasting ways that promote a better overall future self. Only you can change your own personal destiny.

CHAPTER 5

RECOGNIZE THE SKILLS YOU NEED TO BEGIN BUILDING TO ACHIEVE SUCCESS

There is a power people have that often lies dormant in their subconscious mind. Yet this power could turn their life around, if only they knew how to use it. This article describes this mysterious power and shows how to activate it. Warning—this information is not for the faint of heart. Also, when using this power, you must take sole responsibility for everything—good or bad—that happens.

I am only revealing the secrets of this greatest power in stages. I hope that this will help you to better understand and accept these strange ideas. However, you don't have to rely on my words. You can prove or disprove these concepts yourself. You just need to follow the steps shown at the end of this article.

The incredible power of the subconscious mind

The human brain has two separate minds—the conscious mind and the subconscious mind. These two minds have very different purposes. For example, let's see what happens when you open your eyes in the morning. Using your conscious mind, you can observe your surroundings with little or no effort. Meanwhile, your subconscious mind is performing an incredible amount of work. It uses the electrical signals from the optic nerve, together with previously stored information, to resolve these electrical signals into various objects. Then it sends these images, together with any related emotions, to your conscious mind. Your conscious mind, which is not aware of this activity of the subconscious mind, simply receives these images and any related emotions.

"What's the big deal?" you may ask. I'll show you. I'm going to blindfold you and then hand you a bundle of wires. Now using only the electrical signals from this bundle of wires identify the objects in front of you. While we're at it, tell me if any of these objects are dangerous or remind you of joyful experiences. Can't do it, can you?

All I want you to understand right now is that your subconscious mind has fantastic abilities, which it performs mostly in secret.

Contrasting the achievers with ordinary people

Before receiving my revelations, I often wondered why people with the same education, intelligence, and (apparent) ambition achieve such different results in life. Some factors might have affected some of these achievers. They might have received help from influential family members. They might have stumbled onto an opportunity and taken advantage of it. Maybe they were just lucky, good looking, or had some secret driving force.

Personally, I vote for the secret driving force. I think people make their own luck. Have you seen pictures of some rich people? A lot of them are just plain ugly. (Well, probably not movie stars or most other entertainers.)

How your beliefs determine your success in life

The beliefs held in your subconscious mind determine how your brain interprets the world around you, and your ability to achieve success in it. Thus, if you believe that a certain goal isn't possible for you, then you probably won't even try for it. So, if you want to know the nature of your own beliefs, just look around at your surroundings. These surroundings are determined by your beliefs. Do you live in a mansion and drive a fancy car? Unless you inherited your money, your beliefs are very empowering. As for any other type of surroundings, well they just reflect your current beliefs. (Did you notice that I said your current beliefs?)

How the achievers obtained their empowering beliefs

In general, people acquire their beliefs from their experiences in childhood. So if you had supportive parents who achieved their own success in life, they probably instilled those empowering beliefs in you. As for everybody else, well you get the picture.

There are other ways that some people might have developed powerful beliefs. Actions can lead people to change their beliefs. Thus, they might have had inspiring goals that they tried for and achieved. They might have been faced with desperate conditions and surmounted them. Maybe they wanted to make their parents or other loved ones proud of their achievements. Maybe they just wanted to be rich, and were willing to do whatever it takes.

How you can develop empowering beliefs

However, I have written this article so that ordinary people can achieve empowering beliefs. This can be accomplished by various means. You can use affirmations to trick your subconscious mind into believing whatever you wish. You can use physical actions to show your subconscious mind that you are a dynamic and forceful person. You can use visualizations to fool your subconscious mind into believing that you are already successful. You may ask, "Isn't this cheating?" Maybe it is in a way, but so what. You certainly aren't hurting anyone else.

Putting empowering beliefs into action

The following roadmap shows how to put empowering beliefs into action in achieving a goal. Use these steps in the order shown. Each step makes the following step easier to accomplish.

Knowing what to do—There's an old saying, "If you don't know where you want to go, you'll probably end up somewhere else." So to start on your journey to success, first decide where you want to go.

You can decide to start a small business, improve your performance at work, take charge of your life, or just get a tough job done. It's all up to you, my friend.

Overcoming any barriers to action—These barriers to action can keep you from trying to improve your life. For example, you may want to try starting your own business, but something is holding you back. Maybe it's a belief buried in your subconscious mind. The belief might be, "Keep in your own place. Don't try to be something better." If this is your problem, the empowering beliefs you instill in your subconscious mind can overcome this barrier to action.

Other barriers to action are a lack of cash, knowledge, resources, or skills. You need to find ways to obtain whatever is needed. For example you could look up "bootstrap methods" on the Internet. You could work for someone to obtain any needed skills. You could read manuals to obtain any needed information.

Taking decisive action—By decisive action, I mean action that is effective. Action that gets the desired results. For starters, I recommend that you complete any planning required. This planning might be a formal work plan that shows the task requirements (such as the desired results), any advance preparations, activities of main task, and final activities. It can be either a one-page summary or a detailed plan that explains all required action steps.

Correcting any problems—(Note: I define a problem as something that you may not recognize right away and may not know how to fix.) Whenever you take on a new or difficult task, you might run into problems. However, solving problems gives you useful experience and self-confidence. When people want a tough job done, they want someone with useful experience. They want someone who has faced up to problems and solved them. Other people probably have faced and solved similar problems. You just need to search for their solutions on the Internet.

People failed to achieve success in many areas due in a large part to the self doubt that consumes and paralyzes them! Sadly this keeps these people from taking the actions required which may not be all that difficult in the first place! So how is it that folks can overcome the doubts that hold them back in order for them to become successful? Well it seems it would be a matter of taking that first step thus beginning the process necessary for people to overcome their own self doubt while ALSO striving toward the success that has eluded them! 3 steps is all it takes but the hardest one for many will be the first one!

Take Action

Often our own doubts are a reflection of insecurities that lead us to believe we can not become successful pursuing certain endeavors! As a result people decide consciously or otherwise not to even try and this always guarantees one thing which is those particular goals will go unfulfilled! The best way to minimize the self doubt that sometimes consumes us is to take action, move forward and focus on what it is you're doing! There's a saying that goes 'idle hands are the devils playground' and this is so true in terms of allowing doubts to fester and grow within us. Get busy, focus your energies in a productive fashion and you'll see how fast those doubts fade into the background!

Acquire Experience

The experience you acquire by taking the actions required to realize any goals and objectives you may have help dissolve any doubtfulness about your abilities. Much like riding a bike, the more you do it the better you become until you get to the point that you forgot your fears of even trying in the first place! Nothing vanquishes your doubts and fears faster than acquiring the skills necessary through actual hands on experience!

Been There, Done That

Now that you've developed the skills you formerly did not have by actually taking action you've also developed self confidence! At this point you've come full circle in terms of removing the root of your self doubt in the first place which was a lack of confidence! The new attitude you have which replaces your old fears is one of 'been there done that' and this is a mindset that will help you tackle new challenges with little hesitation!

Many people fail to achieve success quite frankly because they don't even try due to being consumed with self doubt! People who lack confidence are typically reluctant to take the necessary actions required which may place them in a better position to become successful! So it seems this lack of self confidence is what needs to be overcome and the 3 steps suggested above in most cases will provide the remedy! By taking the actions required people gain more experience, expertise and thereby the confidence needed to become successful! The first step is always the hardest but after that it's pretty much all downhill from there!

CHAPTER 6

MANAGE YOUR TIME AND INCREASE YOUR PRODUCTIVITY

Learning how to manage your time will change your life dramatically. If you feel rushed each day to complete your tasks, exhausted by the early afternoon, and have an overall feeling of not completing much of what you set out to do each day, time management is the way to change everything in a positive way. As an entrepreneur, this is crucial to your success.

We all have the same twenty-four hours each day; it's how we use them that can make all the difference. I will explain some principles here, including the ideas of time awareness, 'prime time' hours, and delegation. These three principles will help you to regain control of your life and achieve everything you are setting out to do, no matter what your background or level of expertise in your chosen field.

In order to manage our time, we must first be aware of where the hours are going each day before we can make any changes. Write down what you are doing each waking hour for three full days. Make sure one of the days is a full work day for you and another is a day away from work so that you can get a more accurate reading. You already have a feel for where your time is going, but writing it down is a powerful way to see what needs to change. When I first did this several years ago it turned out I was spending about fifteen hours each week watching television shows. I quickly cut that down to only five hours a week, and increased my exercising by another five hours. That left fine hours that I could devote to building my business.

'Prime time' hours refer to the hours when you are at your best. My best time is in the morning, from about seven to eleven. During this time I do the majority of my writing, my product creation, and working in my online business. I can be so productive during this four hour period that I will accomplishment more than many people might spend in eight hours. You know when you are at your best, so think of this as your 'prime time'.

Delegation did not come easily to me. I was used to doing everything myself, and believed that if you wanted something done right you pretty much had to do it yourself. This simply isn't true. Finding the right people to help you in your personal and business life will increase your productivity tenfold.

Learn how to manage your time and the world becomes more joyful, you have time to smell the flowers, and you will most certainly increase your bottom line.

Remember that the reason to learn more about time management is to give you both the time and financial freedom to live the life you choose. Download free training on time management by visiting Time Management for Entrepreneurs to learn how to manage your time as an entrepreneur to build a profitable online business.

What is more important to you, Time or Money? Well, once you have spent your money, you can always earn more, but once you have spent your time, it is gone forever.

How you invest your time is one of the biggest keys to your business and personal success. Have you actually thought about how you use your time on a daily basis and how it could be used more effectively and efficiently? This is the first step to increasing the profit in your business.

It comes down to you, your priorities, and your mindset. Its about looking at what you role is in your business and asking what you can do to facilitate getting more done with less.

Do you know how to reduce the time you spend in your business while increasing your income at the same time?

You might even say that this is impossible, or even financial suicide. But this is actually the first thing you need to do if you want your business to grow and to increase its profitability.

To reduce the amount of time you spend in your business, you must consider your time an investment, that is, investing your time, rather than spending it. You also need to understand that there is a rate of return on the amount of time you invest, just like if you invested $1000 in shares, you would expect a return on your investment. If your time were worth $100 per hour, and you were investing 10 hours of time into your business each day, that's a $1000 investment that you should be seeing a pretty good return on.

Planning and setting goals up front will allow you to use your time wisely and ensure the continued growth of you and your business. You should calculate your productivity as a percentage of the total time you spend in your business, and spend more time on those activities that will increase your income and less time on other demanding and unimportant tasks. So often, I have seen business owners doing things in their business that they should not be doing, but they continue to do them because they are comfortable doing it and it is familiar to them. They focus on doing what they know, instead of what they should be doing, but don't really want to do.

If you have ever been guilty of this, then I urge you to ask yourself this question:

"Should I focus 10% of my time on a task or have someone else give it 100% of their attention, even if this person is only half as good as me?

After all, which is easier - a 100% improvement in your own productivity, or a 5% improvement in your staff's productivity. To get your business to the stage where it provides you with the lifestyle you want, you need to get paid what you are worth. This means preventing your time from being squandered away on low value, but necessary tasks, and creating and developing a team that can run your business for you. To find out if you are being paid what you are worth try this simple exercise:

Calculate the total hours you work in your business each week

Write down the amount that you pay yourself from your business each week and divide that by the total number of hours worked and this will give you your hourly rate.

Is it what you expected? Is it even legal to pay someone that much, who has all your knowledge and experience? The time is now to change. Make the effort to change what you are doing, stop doing low priority, low value but necessary tasks - get someone else to do them, and invest your time in the activities that will directly increase your income and grow your business.

CHAPTER 7

CONTROL YOUR THOUGHTS AND DEVELOP AN UNSTOPPABLE MINDSET

We all have conscious thoughts, subconscious thoughts and a self-image of ourselves in our thoughts. These three separate thought processes are located in separate parts of our brains and in combination they control our lives.

Why is all of this important? Because we become what we think about on all three levels. All three streams of thought must be in harmony for us to lead amazing lives.

Your Conscious Mind: Most of us focus primarily on our conscious thoughts. We all have many goals and ambitions that we think about. Yet, a very small percentage of people ever achieve all their goals and ambitions. There are many reasons why: Lack of vision, lack of purpose, lack of planning, lack of focus, lack of proper actions, lack of drive, lack of patience, lack of persistence, lack of knowledge, lack of learning, lack of skills, lack of resourcefulness, lack of diligent work, lack of effort, lack of energy, etc.

But the primary, overriding reason is mindset. Our mindset controls whether we possess or whether we lack all of the ingredients above. And beyond that, our mindset is actually three different mindsets that function independently of each other.

Think about it: How many people do you know who always appear to have one foot on the accelerator and one foot on the brake in running their lives? Their conscious minds tell them: go, go, go, and do, do, do... And their subconscious minds are telling them: but, but, but, and what if, what if, what if... Have you ever seen a car operate effectively when the driver has one foot on the gas and one foot on the brake? Have you ever seen anyone achieve anything meaningful with one foot on the gas and one foot on the brake? No, no, no to both examples!

Yet that is exactly how most people move through life. They get excited about going somewhere exciting, and then they hit the gas, and then put the other foot on the brake. No wonder they never get anywhere they want to go.

Most of us have done this at one time or another, and this really explains our lack of desired results. Everyone fails now and then, that's just part of the process, and this explains why miss on getting what we desire.

However, some people do it chronically. In fact, some fail almost all of the time, and this leads to chronic failure.

You can tell your conscious mind anything you like. You can dream, plan, commit and take action, but if your subconscious mind slows you down, or even worse, if it stops you, this type of subconscious self-sabotage will prevent you from living your dreams.

Your conscious thoughts are what you tell yourself. It is what you think, plan, write, say and willfully focus on. To control your conscious mind, you must put into writing a very detailed business plan on how you will achieve what you desire and by when. Then you need to look at it and follow it weekly and daily.

Your Subconscious Mind: Your subconscious thoughts are what you really believe, or what you fear. It is your back seat driver, your head trash, your negative self-talk, your doubts and uncertainties. It is the all of the stupid questions you ask yourself when you are daydreaming. It is the part of your brain that focuses on the past instead of the present or the future. It is the part of your brain that tends to focus on negatives instead of positives.

To succeed in life, you really need to believe what you are consciously telling yourself. You need to believe it in your subconscious mind. Until you fully believe, you will ultimately self-sabotage.

Just because most of your thinking is subconscious does not mean that you have no control over it. You absolutely do have control over your subconscious thoughts. You control them by deciding to believe in the positives, not the negatives. When you overcome your fears and doubts by focusing on the many reasons why you want something, you will attract, adapt and create a bright future. You will become unstoppable!

Your Self-Image: Now, let's talk about your self-image. This is the third part of your thinking that is critical for your success.

The steps to achieve success in anything are See, Be, Do and Have. To have what we want in life, we need to see it first. We must visualize it, plan it, write it and see it happening for us. Then we need to believe, and actually be the type of person that is necessary to achieve and have what we desire. Then we must do anything and everything that is required for our success. We need to allow our success and receive it and actually have what we want in life. We See, Be, Do and Have.

Think about the origin of the words: believe, behave and become. Believe is Be + Live. You be it and you will live it. Behave is Be + Have. You be it and you will have it. Become is Be + Come. You be it and it will come.

What is the root cause in all of these words? It's Be. You have to Be who you desire before you can get what you desire. To Be really means to Believe it and Live it.

Who are you being? Examine who you are being. If you want to be a successful entrepreneur, are you being the type of person who is a successful entrepreneur? Are you modeling successful entrepreneurs and being the same type of person and doing what they do? Or are you modeling people who are failing and being a failing entrepreneur? Every business has some huge successes and some huge failures. The characteristics of the individuals in each category are distinctive and unique. Failures are being failures and successful individuals are being successful individuals.

This is where self-image comes in. Who are you? Who do you see yourself as? In your own mind, who are you being? Are you being a huge success or a failure? You cannot succeed until you become in your mind the type of person who succeeds. You will attract what you have in your mind.

In order to become the type of person who succeeds much more often than fails, your self-image is critical. If you see yourself as a failure, you will eventually fail. If you see yourself as a success, you will eventually succeed. It's just as simple as that. And yet, very few of us are aware of exactly what our thoughts and beliefs are regarding our own self-image.

Love the person in your mirror. See yourself as the person you want to be. Never look to the past. It's a waste of time and energy. Look to the future and focus on the present. See yourself as the person you want to be. Be that person daily - meaning think, feel and act like that successful person, and you will soon become that person. You will eventually have what successful people have. Create your future self in your mind and then step into being that person.

Thought Control: Now, the final question may be: How do I control all of my thoughts? I know what I want in life. I am willing to go for it. I really want it, and yet I am struggling. How do I control my complete mindset? I know I can control my conscious thoughts, but how do I control my subconscious thoughts and my thoughts of self-image?

The answer is to take control. If you think you have no control over your life and your future and you are destined for something you have no control over, you are absolutely wrong! You do have control over everything! That's the way the Universe and the Higher Power have designed it. We have control over our lives and our futures!

What is your purpose and what is your passion? It is what you decide it is. What is your future? It is what you decide it is. You can choose and decide. It's as simple as that. You have the power, if you choose to use it. hrough many years of studying the habits of successful people I've come to the conclusion that we all have a natural destiny to grow, to succeed, to prosper and to find happiness during our stay here on earth.

No one intended for us to truly fail. The true sense of failure means giving up without ever trying again to realize your dream. If you truly develop a new meaning of failure you will begin to develop the characteristics of faith, discipline, perseverance, unstoppable fear and persistence.

We were all blessed with certain 'raw' resources that are necessary to move forward. These resources include our imagination, ideas and undeveloped intellectual capacity. This capacity that was given to us is without limitations. The only limitations we have in our life are the limits to fully grasp the idea of our unlimited nature.

It takes effort to believe in a cause. It takes effort to continue on when our results tell us to give up. It takes effort to feel happy about everything that happens to us including the joy and sorrows of our life. However, on the other side, it takes no effort to fail. It takes very little to allow the slowly deteriorating attitude about ourselves, our present and our future. There are few things in our life that we have total control over. One of them happens to be our attitude. Unfortunately, most people are led to believe that we have no control over our attitude.

Through our attitude we can decide to read or not to read. Through our attitude we can decide to try or give up, procrastinate or act. Through our attitude we can blame ourselves for our failure or thoughtlessly blame others. Our attitude can determine whether we lie or tell the truth, advance or recede and of course, whether we succeed or fail.

We are unfinished human beings. By that I mean, there are so many bridges yet to be built, places yet to be discovered, talents yet to be developed and nurtured, new books yet to be written. Your attitude will determine your choices and your choices will determine your results. All that we are and all that we become is left up to us.

Our lives are not determined by what happens to us but by how we react to what happens, not by what life brings to us, but by the attitude we bring to life. A positive attitude causes a chain reaction of positive thoughts, events, and outcomes.

The key to your better future is left up to you.

A positive mental outlook can help you achieve optimal success. Having a positive mental attitude helps you better cope with life's challenges. When life puts you to the test, a positive attitude can help you find your inner strength and overcome adversity. Your positive attitude just might be your winning edge. A study by Harvard University showed that 85% of the reasons for success and accomplishment were because of attitude and only 15% because of technical knowledge and expertise. What this study demonstrates is that it doesn't always matter if you have the tools, skills, knowledge, or resources, the right mental attitude can get you through tough times and help you come out on top.

On the other hand, if you have an attitude filled with a negative perspective it will make everything in your life much harder. Ask any Olympic athlete why they won their event. They'll tell you that they expected to win and that is why they won. This is a great lesson for us all. You can't win when you go into the contest prepared to lose! If you expect to do well, if you have a positive, expecting the best attitude, your winning thoughts will help you succeed.

In order to make your mind think consistent, positive, winning thoughts you need training. Just as we train our bodies for peak performance, we must also train our minds by coaching ourselves to think winning thoughts. You need to put yourself on a mental positive fitness regimen.

One of they ways to do this is by using the NLP technique of "re-framing". Re-framing is looking at challenges as opportunities instead of obstacles. A problem is only a problem if you allow it to be one. A challenge, on the other hand, is an opportunity to learn and improve. So if you search for solutions, you'll find them.

As you internalize this mindset, you'll develop a winning attitude for a lifetime. This attitude will help you reap the rewards of true success and happiness.

CHAPTER 8

MAKE BETTER DECISIONS, EVEN IF UNDER PRESSURE.

We all have to make big decisions at certain points in our lives. If you operate your own business, then making big decisions is likely to be a familiar task. But even those who don't have their own businesses find themselves at various levels of their lives forced to make big decisions.

Let's face it; making a big decision is not easy. It can be painful most of the times. That's because big decisions affect important areas in our lives. Whether it be our business, health, lifestyle, or any other area.

One particular tactic that I find helpful in some cases is creating a space between me and the decision I have to make for a short period of time. Now, you sure don't need to waste a lot of time in the processes of making the decision, especially if it's a small one. But the point of this technique is to assist you in making big decisions that can impose a lot of pressure on you.

Why Is the Space Important?

How do you usually react to stressful situations? That's right, by being stressed out. Stress is the natural reaction to any kind of demand, whether it's physical, mental, emotional, etc. And when having to make a big decision, there's a huge demand that's imposed right on your shoulders.

By creating a space between yourself and the situation, you first dissociate yourself from the stressful state. This one benefit is extremely important as your brain's performance tends to worsen and get less effective when its under pressure.

When you're not stressed out, you're decision making abilities and skills are more accessible and more easily exploited. When you are stress-free, you tend to think clearer and with much more effectiveness.

How to Create the Space?

When it comes to creating the actual space there are no right ways and wrong ways of doing it. That's because there's no one space that must be used by all individuals.

Please notice that the "space" here can be anything, like, doing an activity, being somewhere, doing nothing, etc.

The features of a good space:

✓ Enjoyable
✓ Effortless
✓ Not too long
✓ Make you feel good

So let's apply those features to a solid and practical example. Suppose you own a medium-sized business and have to make a critical decision about which supplier to sign a contract with. This decision is very important because it will have direct impact on the business's costs for years to come. But now you're too tired and stressed and you know that when you make decisions in such a state you tend to make lousy decisions. So, what do you do? You think for a bit and then decide to wait until you're feeling better, and to do something relaxing for that purpose. You then hurry home, take a great hot bath that makes your muscles relax and get rid of the all-day tension. During the bath, when you're feeling totally relaxed and calm, a great idea pops up in your mind that you can use to make your decision.

And even if no ideas pop up in you mind, you'll still benefit from this necessary space between you and the situation you're in, because when you get back to work you'll be much more capable of making a good decision.

Of course you can apply this to many aspects of your life. For example, if you're a student who wants to create a good studying schedule for the exams, you'd better not do that when you're feeling all the exams pressure over your shoulders, because you're most likely to come up with a crappy schedule that do you more harm than good.

Instead, go do something fun. Go play some video games, hang out with friends, or whatever that helps you relieve stress and come back to work.

I know you're too smart to need to be told not to waste too much time on this. Obviously, half an our of video games playing would be more than enough to make you feel good, if videos games relax you of course, because for some people video games is a true source of stress. It all depends on what you like and makes your tension loosen.

Our minds are always into thinking about it - Decisions and more Decisions to make. Our everyday lives are full of it, small mundane ones to large life-changing types. To have the right to choose and make decisions are important to our well-being, and is central to us being an Individual. However, sometimes we just make decisions so bad that make us very unhappy or live with lifelong regrets.

Over the few decades, scientists, neurologists and psychologists are looking into the possible mental processes and signals that may affect our decision makings. Here i distilled some of the findings and will share with you 8 simple ways to make better decisions towards your success.

A) Danger of Social Pressure

Everyone of us would like to think of our-self as a single-minded individual and have a clear say of what we want, but in fact no one is immune to Social Pressure. Many studies have shown that human succumb to social pressure especially at extreme conditions.

We do have ways to avoid the the danger of Social Pressure. At anytime that you suspect that your decisions are based on what your superior or senior wanted, step back and re-group your thoughts. When you are in a group and everyone agree on a certain thing, don't assume they are right and go along. Step back and ask yourself if this is true, and if not - be the one to oppose and share with them your thoughts and reasoning. Beware of situations when you have little responsibilities because that is where you are most likely to make irresponsible decisions and feedback.

B) Do Not Fear Consequences

Every decision that we are making usually involves predicting the future, be it choosing who to date and marry, changing of jobs or what course to study. We normally try to imagine how our choices will make us feel, and we usually go for the option we think will make us the happiest. The problem is that we are not that good in this type of affectionate forecasting.

We have too often overestimate the impact of our decision outcomes, both good and bad. In fact the outcomes of most events are less intense and briefer than most people thought. A major factor is due to Lost Aversion, where we feel that A Loss will hurt more than A Gain will make us happy.

Our solution? Instead of imagining how a outcome can make us feel, we should try to find someone who has made the same choice before and see how they felt. Is is important to understand that whatever the future holds, it will probably hurt or please you less than you have imagined.

C) Go with Gut-Feeling

Sometimes an instinctive and instantaneous choice might be as good as a decision that requires much time to conjure. We make judgements about a persons' competence, aggressiveness and trustworthiness within the 100 milliseconds of seeing a new face. Given a longer time to look (up to 1 -2 second), researchers found that observers hardly revised their views, but only become more confident in their snapshots decisions. Something you are familiar isn't it?

Some would argue that extra information can help you to make rational decisions. Yet many times, the more information you have, the better off you may be going with instincts. Practice with cautious and experience perhaps.

D) Emotions Consideration

We all think that emotions are the enemy of decision making, but in fact they are integral to it. Neurologist studies show that whenever we make a decisions, the brains' emotional centre is active. Our brain stores emotional memories of past choices, which we use to inform present decisions. This is detrimental as making choices under the influence of an emotion can seriously affect the outcome of it.

Personal experience shows that when we are angry or nervous, we are more prone to accepting the first thing that we are being offered rather than consider other options that are available. Anger and nervousness seems to make us risk-prone and impetuous. All emotions affect our thinking and motivation, so it may be best to avoid making decisions under such circumstances.

Sadness on the other hand, surprisingly, seems to help us make better decisions. When we are sad, we seems to take time to consider the various options on offer, and ended up making better decisions. There are reports that indicated depressed people have the most realistic take on this world.

E) Understand that Irrelevant Figures affect our brain

Our decisions are easily attached to irrelevant facts and figures that we come across. Every-time when we see something that marked "reduced price", "end-of-year sale", "moving-out sale" in a shop, we lost our senses for making decisions. The original price serves as an anchor against which we compare the discounted price and we make it look like a great bargain even if in absolute terms it's expensive. This is very difficult to break. One way is to resist the temptation and spend sometime looking around for similar products or services.

F) Looking from the other angle

We prefer options that seems to offer some gains and detest those that seems to involve losses. This is a common weakness in us that marketing department of products and service tend to exploit. We would rather a product that indicate "80% fat free" than another that shows "20% fat".

It is tough to ignore such effects but it is important to at least know that such biases is around. Better education and experience will come in to negate this effect. But for now - we can avoid it by looking at other angle.

G) Be Adaptable and Flexible

All the success coach and motivation guru always tells us to have perseverance and be strong to drive the project or ideas through. This is not wrong, but i believe they did not mention that we should persevere but be open, adaptable and flexible at all times. We need to be realistic.

The notion is that the more we invest in something, the more commitment we feel towards it. The investment need not be in financial form. Who has not persevered with a tedious thick book, and yet find it not interesting at all? Does this scenario sounds familiar to you? Always remind yourself that the past is the past. It is alright to move on, as there might be better things ahead of it, compared to the current settings. If at the time of considering whether to end a book or a project, that you would not initiate now if given a choice, then it's probably not a good idea to continue. Scrape it and start something new and refreshing.

H) Limit Your Options

We might think more choice is better. But consider this - Let say you are trying to get a packet of crackers for you son. Would you be happier to choose from a selection of 10 or a selection of 30? This is commonly known as the paradox of Choice. In fact more choices is not always good. Sometimes, less choice is better.

More choices requires more information processing skills and the process can be time-consuming and confusing. Greater choice also increases the chances of making mistakes, so we will easily feel less satisfied due to the fear that we have chosen a wrong option and missed a better opportunity.

This paradox of Choice is worst for people that examine all options before making up their minds. They spend whole lots of time and energy trying to find the Best Solution. Those people that tend to choose the first option that meets their requirements suffer least. If we are out to find a 'good enough' answer, a lot of the pressure is off and task of choosing something in the avalanche of choices becomes manageable. Thus, instead of searching for your ideal Hand-phone, ask a friend if he is happy with his. If he is, it will probably work for you too. Even in situations when a choice seems far too important to simply choose it, try to limit the number of options.

I) Avoid Procrastination

For cases where time permit us to slowly come up with the decisions, it might be detrimental if we do not keep it in check. By being complacent and only visiting on surface the problem is not good for us. We should avoid procrastination and think and of the possible options that we have and jot it down. In this case, we have a certain "number of options" in our list and can easily filter out one at a time as each day passes. This ensures that our mind is clear of our action

CHAPTER 9

KEEP YOURSELF FOCUSED ON YOUR GOALS, EVEN BETWEEN DISTRACTIONS

We ask every leader we work with what they would do more of, better, or more often when they look back on their career, and the top answer is "Focus." When asked how they would do that, they answer that they would be even more goal oriented than they had been. In their opinion, goals create focus that creates accomplishment. With so many demands intruding or attempting to intrude on their attention and energies, goals that create focus are their firewall, and their primary path to success.

Given that so many highly successful people look to goals for focus, why is it that so many organizations and people can't state their personal goals or the goals of their organization - let alone how their personal goals align with their organizational goals?

One reason given is time - "We don't have time for that - we're too busy. " Another reason (read excuse) given is the belief that an individual has no control over their future - too many things outside a person's control can cause things to change, so just go with the flow.

It turns out that most people spend more time focused on planning a two week vacation than they do planning their career. I suspect that's because planning a vacation is controllable, pleasant, and near term - it's easy to focus on it.

But to succeed and prosper, it's vitally important to have a personal set of goals. - they keep us in the game - whatever game is being played. And personal goals that closely align with organizational goals create a tremendous amount of energy, commitment and focus.

Personal goals are even more important when organizational goals don't exist, or aren't expressed, or exist in name only. It's very tempting in those cases to simply give in to the flow of the day to day, and go with whatever comes along - with little if any focus.

Goals help balance the very human tendency to be distracted by the pressing, in - your - face things that happen every day - it's called being "flexible." Flexibility can be a strength, but it can also be a weakness - when flexing becomes a habit and we look back and see that flexing took us far away from where we wanted to be or needed to be.

A friend shared a joke with me that illustrates that point - "Inside every 65 year old is a 40 year old wondering what the hell happened?"

Focus is the difference between wondering what the hell happened, and landing where you wanted to land. It's the difference between throwing a touchdown pass - or throwing a superball - and watching it bounce every which way - with high energy, but with no idea where it will land - and what good - or damage - it will do.

Here are six steps to create focus:

1 - Write down where you want to be in one month, six months, one year, three years and five years. I know, it sounds like a lot of work. It is. But I can tell you from personal experience that those time frames will blow right past you if you don't take the time to plan them now. And you'll end up like that 65 year old wondering what happened.

2 - Define how your source of income - your job - your profession - fits into your own goals. How do your work goals fit in with your personal goals? Are they the same? How can they come together in the near term to provide long term benefit? The closer your personal goals align with the goals of your organization or profession, the better your chances of accomplishing them. This is the key to focus - being convinced and directed to success through goals that embrace you personally and professionally.

3 - Start with short term goals, but with the end in mind. Weekly, monthly, quarterly. Define the top 3 to 5 things that you need to do now to get you to where you want to be. No more than 3 to 5 - and 5 is a stretch. Remember, you can only really focus on doing one thing at

a time. There is no more powerful way to become discouraged than to "over goal" yourself at this stage.

4 - Express your goals in positive terms. Express your goals in terms of what you want to achieve as opposed to what you want to avoid or get rid of. Optimism loves positive outcomes - work to think in those terms.

5 - Define your goals using the SMART formula - Specific, Measurable, Attainable, Realistic and Time - framed.

6 - Keep track. Hold yourself accountable. Review your goals at least weekly. Carry them with you wherever you go. Make them part of your thinking. Make a habit of reciting your goals and the outcomes of achieving them. Make them your way of life. And when they need to be revised - and that will happen often - just do it.

If you're feeling frustrated and busy and not sure where you're going, start this process today. It isn't easy. It requires personal discipline. It requires faith in yourself. But the rewards of a sense of purpose, focus and freedom are worth the effort. And when you look back in a few weeks to a few months, you'll be surprised at how far you've come, and making goals the cornerstone of focus will become a habit - a habit of success.

How often have you set out to achieve a goal,create changes, make improvements only to find that you end up getting distracted and never complete what you set out to do?

Getting your mind to focus and concentrate on what you want, so that it finds solutions instead of focusing on the problems is usually the difference between success and failure

Unfortunately most people spend a good part of their life reacting to situations, and focus on what's wrong in their lives - which only leads to creating and attracting more of what they don't want.

In order to achieve success you have to discipline and train the mind so that you send the right messages to your subconscious mind - which then creates or attracts exactly what you want.

Disciplining your mind so that it is focused on your goals is crucial to your success.

If your mind is not trained to focus on finding ways to help you accomplish the life that you want - then you really have no chance at success.

Your mind is a direct link to your subconscious mind, if your mind is focused on your goals, and is used to finding ways to help you achieve those goals - then your subconscious mind will also be focused on those goals and will attract the

situations and opportunities for you to achieve the success you want.

When you're focused you'll take the right action to achieve those goals. The minute you get distracted for a prolonged period - you lose sight of your objective and fail to accomplish those goals.

Think of it this way, you're riding in a car driven by your personal driver and every time your driver asks you where you want to go you simply say: "I don't know. Where ever you want to go is fine with me." Then when your driver takes you to the place of his choice you complain and say: "I don't want to be here, take me somewhere else." And again you say you don't know where you want to go - leaving it to your driver to go where he chooses, and you continue to end up where you don't want to be -because you can't decide or focus on where you want to go.

If you don't train your mind to focus on what you want then your subconscious mind cannot create the situations that will help you achieve your goals and in the end your subconscious gets confused - thus creating more confusion for you—and you end up exactly where you don't want to be.

Let's go back to the example of your personal driver. Wouldn't it be a lot easier and more comfortable if you told your driver where you wanted to go -or even better - your driver know your movement in other to go ahead of time. The latter will never happen if you don't train your driver or work with him to develop the ability to go where you want when you want.

Your subconscious mind is your driver - give it the right instructions and it will guide you to the situations, people and events that will help you achieve your goals - it will take you exactly where you want to go.

When you have your mind focused on your goals you find solutions and discover opportunities to help you achieve your goals. Your responsibility is to follow up on these opportunities. Decide what you want to achieve. Keep your mind focused on what you want to happen. Send the right messages to your subconscious mind.

Give your driver the right instructions and you'll start creating the life you want.

How do you train your mind?

The first step is to get your mind to stop doing what it is used to doing - or break the pattern that you've been following for so long. This will require some effort - but remember - once you get your mind to work differently you'll be able to live the life you want and enjoy tremendous success.

To begin - follow your normal routine, then when you see yourself getting distracted and not following up on things that you wanted to do break the pattern.

You can start by following up on what you had planned to do, you can create a list and follow up with it regularly to see if you're on track. One thing that always works is to think about your goals every morning. As you lie in bed, think about your goals and think about what you can do to achieve them during the day.

Do this everyday.

If you find you constantly say: "I don't know what to do to achieve my goals." Then you're not looking for answers in the right place. Take a look at what other people have done to achieve similar goals and see if you can follow the same process. For example: If you want to make more money take a look at someone else who has made a lot of money and see what they've done.

Can you follow their process? Maybe you can even talk to them about the process? If you want to meet someone and be in a healthy relationship, talk to a friend who is in a successful relationship and find out what they did.

By doing the above exercises you train your mind to focus on finding solutions while at the same time you direct your subconscious mind to create the opportunities for you to succeed.

Another important event takes place as well - you begin to create a new pattern of thinking and thus you start to train the mind to work differently. You're now telling your driver where you want to go. So not only do you begin creating what you want - you also end the confusion and stop attracting what you don't want.

You're not going to magically get your mind to focus or concentrate without taking some form of action - without consciously forcing it to focus on your goals or what you want.

When you finally do take some action your mind will still resist but as you continue taking action and continue pushing it in a new direction, as you regularly get it to focus on what you want, the resistance will subside.

So what action can you take?

First start with the exercise I just outlined above. Next - meditate. Meditation is one of the best ways to relax and calm your mind while training it to focus better. When you meditate you actually start to clear the clutter that dominates your mind.

There are a number of other techniques that you can work with - but what I've outlined will get you started.

Begin training your mind to work differently. Get your mind to focus on what you want. Feed your subconscious mind the right instructions so that it creates what you want.

Here's a suggestion; the next time you are driving or taking a shower, pay attention to your thoughts. Are these thoughts actually working for your or against you? Would it be better to focus on your goals or keep recycling the negative clutter or junk in your head?

The choice is yours - and taking action is really about taking a small step at a time.

You don't need to spend hours meditating. Even if you simply mediated for 5 or 10

minutes a day you'd be able to increase your ability to concentrate and focus

by a 100-percent within a matter of days! Do it for a few weeks or months and you'll have dramatic results.

CHAPTER 10

BOOST YOUR LEADERSHIP SKILLS

Everyone knows that great leaders are made, not born. However good that statement sounds, we still want to know how we "make" or turn people effective leaders. And other questions need to be answered about the process of leadership development.

So how DO you boost your leadership skills? If you want to improve your ability to lead, where should you focus your attention? Why are certain leadership talents more important than others? To Boost or not to - that's a good question.

Would you want to be a leader with more skills? Yes, especially when you consider the opportunities "more" skills offer you. You would want to effectively plan a strategy or generate purposeful agenda to meet the challenges of your daily situations.

You could employ different skills to encourage your team to perform beyond their ordinary level, bridge the gaps causing low morale in your followers or coach and counsel people who face difficult circumstances. With more skills, you would be better prepared to take action with greater confidence, and you would act more decisively.

At some point you made a conscious decision to become a leader. You have observed and studied and prepared well, and now your leadership opportunity has arrived. You are excited about your prospects and anxious to get started. The burning question thus becomes: What will you do?

There are a number of common attributes that can be fairly used to describe successful leaders. But what particular skills do these leaders demonstrate most often? What do their colleagues and employees typically see from these leaders as they go about their work? Which skills make these leaders consistently high achievers?

In the broader sense, developing leadership is an effective way of enhancing the skill of a person. A company can make arrangement for their employee a leadership training program or an individual can enlist him/her in a leadership training course. Quality leadership is a combination of the right qualities and the right training. Investing in leadership development program will help build your team's leadership fundamentals, that will ensure you are more than likely to have a bright career path ahead of you.

A good coaching program where you get an online leadership certificate will help prepare yourself for facing any challenging situation in a cool and calm way, reshaping your decision making power and boost your personality. You will feel more confident to tackle adversity, hindrances and complexities tactfully. Influential leadership trainers from all over the world share their actual experience with you that will open up your eyes to understand the business world and what it actually demands from an individual.

Participants of the online leadership certificate courses obtain practical knowledge they can make great use of directly to their environment of work. The entire leadership training program is given online and designed in a way that an individual becomes eligible for common leadership and management challenges.

It would be worthwhile for any leader to exhibit the below five leadership skills as a way not only to boost the probability of success, but to cultivate a distinctive tone of excellence and professionalism:

1. Lead with integrity. Live the values you espouse. Every day, every way. Your honesty and sense of fairness will bring trust and credibility over time, and will very likely improve the quality of followership being offered by your employees. Doing the right thing sometimes takes a stiff backbone; don't be seen as one who looks for the path of least resistance. Never lose sight of the fact that men and women of high integrity are particularly valued.

2. See the bigger picture. Leaders look beyond the present and try to understand what the future may hold. Don't make a habit of reacting impulsively, but instead consider the broader scope. Ramifications and consequences, either intended or otherwise, are considerations a

forward-looking leader should routinely attempt to identify, quantify, and balance. Knee-jerk reactions are seldom the best expression of leadership skills.

3. Create an atmosphere of continuous improvement. Skillful leaders understand that comfortable, contented organizations will soon to be lapped and driven to the rear of the pack by the faster and more agile. Continuous improvement has long since moved from slogan to necessity, and leaders who create, drive, and institutionalize such a process stand a far better chance of remaining competitive.

4. Be a team player. Leaders with egos so inflated that they have a hard time acknowledging anyone's contributions and accomplishments but their own will eventually find themselves on an island. And there will be few, if any, volunteers to rescue them. Conversely, a leader who unselfishly listens to and takes advice from others, who distributes credit for the successes, and who takes full responsibility for the shortcomings, will likely never suffer a shortage of dedicated supporters.

5. Make things happen. Be a person of action, of movement, of creativity. Be willing to take a calculated risk for a worthwhile gain. Leaders need accomplishments, they need wins, and above all they have the energy and drive to move the organization forward. Leaders perform, attracting others who perform, and their impact is felt not just in who they are, but most especially in what they do.

CHAPTER 11

DEVELOP YOUR WILLPOWER AND CONNECTION WITH YOUR SPIRITUAL SELF

if you develop your willpower, you can definitely be more successful in life. In fact, the two are directly related. No one can underestimate the power of willpower in helping you achieve your goals.

Even though we hear often about the importance of good education, in fact, it's not the lack of it that causes most failure. There are many people with little to no formal education who have in fact become millionaires, while many people with Ivy League degrees muddle along in dead-end jobs, or worse. In fact, it's willpower, not a degree per se, that can determine your chances for success.

Of course, basic education is important; simply because it helps you get along in society. However, just as important and perhaps more important is the fact that you see yourself succeeding and will pick yourself up and try again to matter how many times you fail in the first place. It's a proven fact that both Henry Ford and Harry Truman had failed in everything they had done before they established their particular places in history: Ford with his invention of the assembly line and subsequent mass-produced and cheaply built car, and Harry Truman first as a senator and with a brief stint as Vice President, finally becoming President of the United States.

Just as with any type of skill, willpower and determination take time and practice to develop. Just as you train the physical body for a marathon, so, too, you see yourself succeeding in your mind. As you continue these visualizations, reality meets imagination halfway. Providing you've laid the groundwork before as well, success is almost inevitable.

In essence, self-mastery of your mind must become a habit. Practice daily and gradually build up confidence and resistance to failure, even as you keep your eyes open and maintain common sense so as not to be foolhardy. With self-mastery comes accomplishment, and ultimately, success.

In fact, you don't need to be a genius to succeed. Most people are not born Albert Einstein or Wolfgang Amadeus Mozart. Most people have ordinary IQs, but what they have that the next person doesn't is determination and the willingness to practice until perfect. Keep trying, even if drudgery sets in short-term. It's the practice that makes the difference.

In fact, Henry Ward Beecher was a master of accomplishment, and when asked what his secret was, he said, "I don't do more, but less than others. They do all their work three times. Once in anticipation, once in actuality, and once in rumination. I do mine in actuality alone, so I end up doing things just once."

Basically, Beecher could concentrate perfectly on what he was doing at any given moment without distraction. Most of us, try though we might at least distracted somewhat with random thoughts, worry about another project other than the one we're working on, or other mind distractions we would better do without in a given moment. If you put those aside until such time as you can take care of them with similar singular focus, it's much more efficient and your success is much more guaranteed. Therefore, one of the biggest secrets to being successful is the ability to focus all of your attention on one thing at a time.

A note about worry: Even though worry seems like it's inevitable, in fact, it's mostly a habit. Most things you worry about will never happen, which makes this a wasted practice; and if, in fact, a worry does in fact manifest in reality, there's usually nothing you could have done about it before hand. If you simply can't put your worries to rest, them down on a piece of paper, tuck it away, and promise yourself that you will focus on those worries with your full attention in their own time. With this done, you can free yourself of the worries that would normally plague you and focus on the task at hand. If you don't do this, worry will only drain you, for no good effect. It can suck your energy away for no good reason, reduce your chances of success and make you and those around you miserable.

By focusing on a given task at a time, you exponentially increase your chances of success and what you can achieve. As soon as you can learn this, the better, because it's a sure way to overcome one very big hurdle that can slow you down and prevent you from attaining the success you deserve.

"I'm so lonely that I can't stand it." "I just have to accept that I am going to be alone forever." "What's wrong with me? I can't seem to find anyone to love and will love me back?" These are statements that I hear over and over again from the souls on the couch across from me. Emotional pain pours out like beads of sweat on a sweltering day, permeating the room with the smell of despair. Quick glances upward, faint flickers of hope emitting from their eyes as they look to me for help. I know their pain; been there, done that.

For most people, there is nothing more painful than being single when you want to be married or in a committed relationship. After all, it's supposed to be easy, right? You tell yourself that you're a good person; that you want to love someone and have him or her love you back. You wake longing to create a deeply intimate bond with that someone special and live in the land of Happily Ever After. It is the future, not the here and now that will bring happiness and a sense of contentment.

FEEDING YOUR SPIRITUAL SELF

"Why can't I find someone to be in a relationship with?" a young lady ponders.

"What about your relationship with your spiritual self?" I ask.

"I don't give that a lot of thought or attention. I am too busy looking for that one person who will be my soul mate to spend time thinking about that. I don't even know how to think about my spiritual self. And, I don't have the time."

It's curious how people expect to create a great relationship with another person when they don't have a great relationship with their Spiritual Self. Feeding the soul is where the journey to creating a dream relationship starts. It is about the here and now, not a fairy tale of the future. Connecting to mindfulness is an important step in living in the here and now; it starts you on a trek of moving away from pain and toward peace and tranquility.

Mindfulness is the act of observing your moment to moment experience and marinating it in kindness. It is about focusing your attention on what is happening in the moment; what you are feeling and thinking in any moment in time. It is being in a stance of openness, where acceptance and non-judgment allow curiosity to flourish. Being curious is critical, as it puts us in a state of seeking wisdom, one of the more valuable things in the universe (intimacy and deep love being the most valuable).

"Have you ever thought about assessing situations without tagging on a judgment?" I ask.

"What do you mean?"

"For example, simply saying 'What I'm doing isn't working for me' and stopping there rather than adding on 'because I'm a loser?'"

"No. Not really. Look at my life. It is nothing like I dreamt it would be. I am a loser!"

Assessing without judging is a critical component of mindfulness. It allows us to look at our morals, values, and belief systems from a perspective of what is working and what is not without poisoning the food (thoughts) that we feed our Soul. Judgment is toxic. Non-judgment is nourishing and leads to enlightenment, empowerment, and transformation.

Mindfulness allows us to look at our spiritual Self and provides the opportunity to feed it a nine course meal. By its very nature it is an act of self love and acceptance. It allows us to look for and create validation from within, rather than looking for it from outside sources.

When we create internal validation, we are in a creative stance which we can control. We fuel our spiritual self and create self love and positive mental states of mind like self acceptance. We walk with life in our gait and radiate out warmth, which is attractive. It creates connections. When we look for validation from outside sources, we are in a desperate stance, we have no control, and we feed negative mental states of mind like Fear. We walk as if the weight of the world is on our shoulders. It is cold and pushes others away. It creates loneliness.

As you continue on your journey to create a dream relationship, remember to feed your Soul a healthy diet of love, warmth, mindfulness, self acceptance, and hope and do it from a non-judgmental stance. Make a promise to your spiritual Self that you will never starve it or poison it again with negative thoughts which contain no nutritional value. In doing so, you will radiate and attract others in a way that you have never experienced.

CHAPTER 12

USE YOUR MIND TO ITS FULL POTENTIAL

Do you want to increase the power of your mind? Many believe that the full potential of the human mind is not totally reached.

In fact, studies show that only a small percentage of the brain is being utilized by the individual. It is for this reason that many psychologists became so confounded about the mental processes thus, they become keen on how to make it reach its full capabilities.

Then came the study about the use of mind control which involves the subconscious mind.

How to develop a powerful mind?

Developing a powerful mind requires more than just motivational talks or even personality development seminars. It requires something more powerful like the use of mind control.

Though it has been a subject for debate in the past years, it remains to be one of the personality development methods that interest many today. In the past years, the use of mind persuasion has a negative connotation as the concept is said to have originated during the war period as brainwashing techniques were said to be used in the army to generate utmost obedience.

But nowadays, mind control is viewed in a more positive way as studies show its effectiveness in the holistic development of an individual.

The use of mind control as a way of enhancing the capabilities of the human mind requires a different kind of persuasion. This process speaks not only to the conscious part of your brain but to the subconscious mind as well.

Normally, the process takes quite some time before results can be evident. It is something that is done only by a trained professional or a licensed psychologist in order to avoid any possible dangers of interfering with the mind. It also involves different methods like sending subliminal messages or persuasion through the use of hypnotism.

What is the role of the subconscious?

In the practice of mind control, the conscious mind is typically the easier part to persuade as the individual makes a conscious effort to develop it. However, in order to reach the full potential of the mind, it is best to enhance the subconscious part as well.

In technical terms, the subconscious mind is defined as something which lies underneath the consciousness. It is said that the subconscious is where an individual's hidden desires, abilities, as well as knowledge lie.

This is the part of the mind that is not fully maximized because not many are aware of its presence. That is why the main goal of the mind control is to speak through the subconscious in order to unleash these hidden capabilities as it can be the only way to reach the full potential of a powerful mind.

How can the subconscious be developed?

It is said that the most effective way to develop the subconscious mind is through frequent repetition or constant reminder.

This means that whatever a person thinks repeatedly and believes wholeheartedly will eventually be picked up by the subconscious and this is what it will end up doing. And so, in order to develop the subconscious mind, it has to be motivated and reminded incessantly.

Say for instance, a woman repeatedly tells her body that she will be promoted at her job. When the subconscious mind becomes aware of the desire, it will do a way to help bring out the potential of the woman in order for her to do well in her job and eventually get promoted.

Are there any benefits?

The use of mind control in developing the conscious and subconscious mind power is said to bring a lot of benefits to an individual's personal growth and development. It is said to help bring out the hidden talents of a person as well as bring about behavioral changes.

It helps build a better character by instilling a positive attitude and outlook as well as boosting the self-esteem of a person.

FIX YOUR EMOTIONAL WEAKNESS

You've heard about Emotional Intelligence (EI). Achieving a high sense of EI skills has shown results for organization and individuals alike in terms of being able to strive in times of uncertainty. However, when we face uncertainties in life and career the problem is that we are never sure as to how long it will last. Life as we know it sometimes throws at us challenges that does not have a quick fix formula and has a tendency to drag us into a rut. It is in these kinds of situations that we need to develop our sense of Emotional Fitness (EF).

Emotional Fitness is a state of being whereby you have the ability to develop a sustained capability and capacity to strife well when the going gets tough. Just like physical fitness is required to run a very long race, you need a sense of emotional fitness when you have got to handle a crisis or some prolonged challenging situation that confronts and confounds you. These situations require an extended period of time to resolve and as such may sap you of your physical and mental energy and may put you in an emotionally bankrupt state.

In these circumstances it would take tremendous emotional energy to remain motivated. This is not an easy state of mind to achieve. However, your ability to ride this wave of uncertainty is what makes you an outstanding person. Abraham Lincoln said: "Let no feeling of discouragement prey upon you and in the end you are sure to succeed."

To achieve this sense of emotional fitness, you need to keep a positive mindset by developing four personal qualities that allow you to be able to live day by day when uncertainty strikes you and work progressively towards an effective method to reduce the tough challenges that you are facing.

The qualities that you should enhance to become emotionally fit are:

Patience

This is perhaps the most important quality to ensure that you develop emotional fitness. There are some things in life that cannot be achieved overnight. If you hit the gym everyday and hope to have a body like Arnold Schwarzenegger in a week, it is just not going to happen. Some people find for 'quick-fixes' like taking steroids and other muscle enhancement medication. But such things come with extreme side effects that may not be a good thing for your body in the long run. What you need is patience in what you are doing. You have to be consistent in what you do and constant in doing it. Likewise, if you have a recurrent problematic situation that saps your emotional energy, be patient and work towards an ideal outcome. There is an ancient Chinese saying that says "it takes many droplets to make the mighty ocean."

Break your problem into small achievable steps and enjoy the little victories every time you solve a small aspect of the problem. These little victories will help you stay focus and motivates you towards handling the problem objectively and effectively.

Develop a sense of Spiritual Centre

Learn to create a sense of spiritual centre in your life. This means accepting who you are and what you can do. In the mad rushing world of today, there is a tendency for us to want things that other people have. This is all well and good, but at what expense? If you can afford a big car then go for it! But if you want the big car because your neighbour or colleague has got one and you want to compete with him, then you are going to be 'hijacked' emotionally as you will come to realize that you don't need the car and you are going to have a tough time servicing the loan. This will definitely sap you of your emotional energy.

You can develop a sense of spirituality by being true to yourself and do things that make you feel good about yourself. Try by writing down the strong points that you have and areas of weaknesses that you wish to overcome. Reason and rationalize with yourself as to what you are doing. Is this the right thing for you to do it? Are you doing it because you want to or because you have to? It may not be easy to always get the answers to these questions. But by asking them you become self-aware and can thus learn to self-regulate. This will then make you a personally competent person.

Engage in Positive Self-Reflections

Positive Self-Reflection means your ability to look at yourself from as a positive and successful person no matter what has happened to you. Sure! There may be things that you might have done that you are not proud or you have had a failed relationship or some form of troubled past. Thinking about things that already happened is not going to make it go away. You need to acknowledge what has happened to you and look at the present and the future. Instead of gravitating towards negativity when tough times confounds you try to think of the many times you were actually successful. Ask yourself how you felt during those successful times. Can you emulate that feeling back to the current situation? Too often we feel trapped by the challenges life throws at us. Although there are no answers to some of the problems that you are experiencing, what you may have, however, are 'alternatives'. These 'alternatives' may help you resolve your problem effectively. You will not be able to identify these 'alternatives' by gravitating yourself towards negative thoughts.

Negative feelings really aren't negative at all when you handle them in a positive way!

The challenge many people face when it comes to unhappy emotions is not wanting to feel them at all, like they are the worst thing ever. Maybe you believe negative feelings are bad, or you can't bear to feel them, or that you are weak, or not a good person if you experience them.

Perhaps you think you are a cry baby, or not a man, or you should be beyond these feelings, or you might even hate yourself for feeling a certain way. None of those are the truth, although you might think they are and therefore you don't want to face them as if they are somehow monstrous.

Many people want a quick fix to get rid of them, or push them aside, or sweep them under the carpet, or pretend they don't exist at all. Doing this isn't seeing or being with them in a positive way; it's avoiding them like they are the plague, which they are not. Negative emotions are far from being the enemy or ogre, but maybe you are being that towards them. Are you?

How are you handling these unwanted and unloved feelings? Are you discarding them like they are trash, or covering them up like a foul smell? It almost makes you sorry for these emotions when you look at them like they are an outcast.

Wouldn't you rather know how to handle them in a positive way than pretend they don't exist or will never surface?

In my experience making believe they aren't there doesn't make them disappear, and quick fixes are only a temporary solution since life is filled with unexpected situations that bring forth these unwelcoming feelings.

You can handle negative emotions in a positive way if you know how, and you won't want to be beating yourself up anymore for experiencing them.

If you were a child and thought something was hiding under your bed, or in your closet, or in the basement, or behind the door or shower curtain, you or your parents might turn the light on and take a look to reassure you that it's okay.

You are going to turn the light on, so to speak, on these misunderstood feelings.

You can start right now by reminding yourself that they aren't bad or awful; they are the opposite feelings to the ones you do like. Negative emotions bring your attention to something to shine the light on so you don't have to remain stuck in fear and darkness.

You can become empowered by, or powerless to your emotions and it's up to you what you do with them.

Choose to see them as ways you can improve your life. They are like messengers, not monsters.Take some time to hear them out; perhaps they have something for you that you just aren't willing to hear or see. Take a closer look.

Ask yourself how you can move through this or if there is anything you need to know. Often unpleasant feelings are really wake up calls and if we were listening each day to our inner voices, instead of our outer ones, a lot of them wouldn't seem so dreadful or even be experienced at all.

Moods are not really the problem, but the way you see and handle them could be. You can continue to avoid them, hate them, push them down or out, but that doesn't mean they aren't there and won't surface at another time.

CHAPTER 13

REACH LONG-TERM PERSEVERANCE

Perseverance is the most important prerequisite of an exemplary life. Perseverance can do several things for you if you develop it as a habit. It has been observed as the only thing that we all need to make the needed difference we had always wanted in the various aspects of our lives. Let us firstly discuss what perseverance means; simply because I know it is beyond the letters. It is only when we understand it in depth that we will be able to realize how potent it is!

Perseverance implies succeeding because you are determined to, not because you are ennobled to it. Great achievers do not sit back and wait for success because they think the world owes them. People that understand perseverance look for circumstance that pleases them, and if possibly they cannot find any, they create one. When you persevere, you already put up with an unlimited success that is not yet announced! You will only be able to feature in that dream future of yours if only you are persistent enough.

Perseverance is also about knowing that life is not one long race, but many short ones in chronological sequence. Each has its own challenges and each day its own cases. You have got to wake up the next day and run again. You understand that the race can ever be the same. To be successful, you must keep the focus. Never consider quitting as an option because the moment you quit doing what you believe in, that minute, you start losing. Perseverance has the potential to turn adversity into advancement. When you think that people hate you because of what you are, you do not have to change and do things their way because they persecute you. Once you are convinced about what you do, then go ahead and be unperturbed about the multitudes. Be more persistent and you will discover that the table will turn to you.

It is only when you persevere, that you will become revered. So work harder.

It is the ultimate aim of a man to plan his future, and this is why long-term investments are so important. If you choose the perfect investment plan, it would mean that when you retire, you will still have the financial freedom that you wished for while investing for a long period. Long-term investments also act as a security measure at a time when you don't have a fixed income anymore and can take care of your health, which is surely not going to be as good as the time you started investing. Therefore making a long-term investment plan is similar to planning one's future.

So, where is the starting point of investing for a long period? There are certain doubts that will surface before investing: What is the best long-term investment plan available? Should one ask for the external help from a financial advisor or go ahead alone? This article gives you certain tips to excel in the long-term investment market.

Setting proper goals: This is common to nearly all types of investing. One should always set reachable goals about the future and then plan the investments likewise. Certain enquiries must be properly addressed before going ahead with the investments. One should know when he/she wants the investment to mature into returns, and the amount he/she expects at the end of the investment period. He/She should also calculate the initial amount to be invested, and the monthly premium that is to be submitted to reach to the goal. Once, the above questions are addressed, it is time to move forward and decide whether a financial advisor is needed or not.

Making the right decision: The investor must understand that it is their hard earned money that they are investing, and one wrong decision would mean a wasted future. Hence, decisions regarding long-term investment should be made after due consultations with concerned people, and after being confident about the firm to which the investment is made. If you take the help of a financial advisor then make sure that they work along with you and under no circumstances should you feel that the money is not under your control.

Regular Follow-up of the investment: Patience and perseverance are the two most important qualities needed in a long-term investor. In spite of the long period, you should never become ignorant about the investment you made, and try to be follow up with the latest happenings in the market. It may be the case that the company that you has your investment is in a crisis. In those testing times, only the alert would be capable to assess the impact properly and make the necessary changes, if any. Hence, ignorance cannot be encouraged in the long-term investment market too!

TRANSFORM YOUR BODY AND MIND

You have the power to transform your life into whatever you want it to become, no matter what your current and past situation entails. All you need to do is remain focused on what your desires are and the dedication to creating your dreams.

The best way to ensure success in transforming your life is to develop a plan and be consistent with your application of putting your plan into practice.

We have the power within us to make our lives any way we want it to be. The only limitations we have in life are the ones we put upon ourselves.

Extreme self-care begins with easing your mind, calming your body, and feeding your soul.

Easing your mind involves being fully present and aware of this very moment. Eliminate the guilt and shame you carry with you from your past and put an end to the unfounded worries about your future. Create more time for gratitude, abundant thinking, a positive attitude and lots of laughterAs important as easing your mind is to your mental health, exercise and relaxation also play a key role in your well being.

Our bodies are marvelous creations that carry us through life. You deserve extreme self care. Just like a beautiful flowering plant, your healthy body needs rich soil and water to create a full and healthy bloom.

Discovering true balance includes creating time to feed your spirit. Nurturing yourself spiritually allows you to ground yourself in your body keeping you anchored, healthy and alive. Caring for the soul includes eliminating the weeds that show up and choke out your natural soulful beauty.

Did you know that your mind is the number one most significant element in the quality of your life? Your mindset determines your success, the quality of your relationships, and your health. You can walk down the street and see rainbows in a puddle of water, or you can see garbage floating there. You have more choice than you can even imagine in determining the quality of your life by transforming the nature of your thoughts. While it's important to accept your thoughts as they are, to treat them as visitors to the "home" within your mind, it's important to understand that you don't need to let these visitors overstay their welcome. In fact you can show them how they can brighten their days by altering the ways they see the world. Let's talk about three habits of mind to avoid and three things to do instead.

Three Habits of Mind to Avoid

• You may feel that you're over powered by your thoughts, that you're the victim of recurring mental "programs" or thought forms. It's harder to deal with your thoughts when you're carrying them like a huge burden in your body and mind. When you have recurring thoughts, it's sometimes difficult to realize that you can do something about them and become more free.

• When something that seems to be "bad" or challenging happens, it's easy to become overly dramatic about it. You might be thinking, "Oh my God, my computer isn't working. This is affecting me to the core. I don't know what to do! My life is ruined" Now this may seem to be an exaggeration, but many people go to very dramatic places when life happens. There are, of course, some extremely difficult events that life brings, but you do have choices as to how you'll deal with them.

• If you have a tendency to act before you've had a chance to think things through, you might be acting too soon. If you can take a moment and be quiet inside, you just might find some solutions inside yourself.

Three Habits of Mind to Adopt

• Realize that you have a lot you can do about your thoughts and that you're not a total victim of them. Yes, recurring thoughts can be troublesome, but you can always go inside yourself and stand back enough to look at your thinking and explore the truth behind your thoughts. There might be another way of looking at your situation if you go inside yourself and ask for it.

• Realize that what seems bad is most often a temporary experience that will change. And even things that seem so terrible are the universe's way of bringing you strength and ultimate inner power.

• Realize that there's a part of you that can guide you on a more positive path. I call it "The Wise Mind." And it's the part of you that knows and understands from a higher perspective. Just ask yourself, "What would my Wise Mind tell me about that?" and listen for an answer. You may be surprised at the guidance and wise solutions that it brings to you.

Quiet time alone restores life balance and raises self-awareness. You go within and connect with something larger than yourself. But how can you hear wisdom from within, if you are never still enough to listen? When possible, walk alone in natural surroundings and reconnect with Earth. You renew body, mind and spirit with time for yourself. Solitude is not a luxury.

Be gentle with yourself and easy about your life. Keep your goals simple, clear and consistent. Single out one area where you want to begin. Choose what feels good to you. Progress in one area almost always leads to progress in others. And commit to sharing your progress with someone else on a regular basis. This practice gives you the best chance for making a change.

You are an infinite choice maker. With each choice you are creating your future. Be aware of what matters the most to you and make conscious choices. With them you are promoting your general well-being. Seek the personal transformation that gives life more meaning. When you make a decision to honor the Mind Body Spirit connection, you grow and thrive. You find more life passion, balance and joy

The best power we all have is the power of decision. Every day we get out of bed and make decisions that influence our lives. From the small decisions to the big ones, they all play a significant factor in how we develop in our lives. When you have made the choice to transform yourself into a better person then you are making one of the most powerful choices of your life. Strengthening the way you perform can support you live a more effective and satisfying life. To change you must first get ready your mind to make sure that your body and actions will adhere to your wishes.

Determine a way to encourage yourself psychologically for an effective change in your life. People attempting to reduce weight should snapshot an image of their shape a few months back from they actually wanted to see them in shape. Whatsoever you have to do to encourage yourself at your inner sslevels do it. You cannot expect to transform if you do not change the way you think. Remove any bad thoughts you have in your mind and focus on the constructive. Positive mind set can support you on long term basis for encouraging you to stick to your goals.

The facts that you want to modify about yourself? Do you want to make a considerable change in your body type? Are you serious in changing your profession? Take a moment and actually imagine about the type of particular person you want to build into. Self improvement is based heavily on the objectives you set up. Plainly summarize your targets to guarantee that you have a clear comprehension of what type of person you desire to change into.

CONCLUSION

Having a positive mental attitude in your life will definitely take you far on your road to success. For this reason, self-awareness, strong commitment and self-disciplines together will contribute to your success in having better self-control and to further your personal development. Self-discipline is the biggest human strength. One of the biggest reason, people fail is due to lack of self-discipline. Willpower can be increased. Sleep well. Practice forgiving yourself. Cultivate mindfulness of your impulses and distractions. Visualize the roadblocks and failures.

Mental toughness is a very important part of life. To be able to complete a task that needs to be done, no matter what your body or your mind is telling you is tough. But once your good at it, nothing can stop you from getting what you want. So how do you get good at it?

People who understand it actually welcome adversity with open arms, because they know that every time something difficult comes up, if they can embrace that and be positive about it, it is a growth opportunity. Those events - handling the unpleasant or the unexpected—develop mental toughness.

Practice connecting with your future self. Hopefully you will be able to use all these techniques to increase your self-discipline. Remember, you have the power with you. You're strong enough to demand the best of yourself. So make the critical decision now to take control of yourself and your own destiny by developing your self-control and self-discipline.

You are the creator of your future! Don't live a life by default, like most people do. Take control! Take charge of your brain! Take control of your life. Create it! Believe it! Do it! Live a life of your choosing! Think it, feel it and believe it. Bring your mindset into harmony. Allow your success. Banish all negative thoughts. Take your foot off the brake. Hit the gas! Live your positive thoughts. Know with certainty that you will attract and create a life and lifestyle that you decide upon. Believe it! And help others along the way. You will brighten your life and brighten the lives of so many people in the world. See it, Believe it, Do it, and Have it! Be the leader! Lead the life you desire! Take control! Train your mind to focus on what you want. Direct your subconscious mind to create the life that you want. Begin attracting the situations and people to help you achieve your goals. Get started today.

Choose your activities carefully and don't juggle too many things at once. It's much more efficient than to focus on one important task at a time than it is to focus on several relatively unimportant ones. In fact, multitasking does not make you more efficient, in most cases. It makes you less efficient. The more you focus, the more you can get done. Most importantly, persistence is what will keep you moving forward and get you to the goals you so desire. Again, focus is the key.

Perseverance means stopping not because you are wearied, but because the task is done. This is because you cannot afford to stop halfway. You are supposed to be result oriented and not a waster of opportunities. You are supposed to enliven and not dissuade others through your dispositions, let your entire life be a fountain of hope for others. You can make these possible if your determination is tough enough.

Prepare a method towards self improvement. Many people that want a beneficial change in their life hire a life coach. Life coach motivates you in every part of life. This person functions as your guide and disciplinary measure should you stray from your path in direction of improvement. It's not necessary that the life coach have to be a professional, your friend or any family member would help you to be your life coach. Most people think what they get in life comes from outside themselves. They never realize that what's coming from the outside is due to what's going on inside. Your state of mind and body determines it all. Even when it doesn't seem to be so.

Take control of your life through your attitude, health habits, and energizing habits.

Just about everyone gets discouraged at some point or another in their lives. Some people try to do something once, and if it doesn't immediately work, they give up right away. Others have a bit more fortitude, and they hang in there for a while longer. Some people just keep on keeping on. They never give up, and finally one day, the rainbow appears, the sun appears in the sky, and the band starts playing - well, maybe not all this, but results begin to take place when they least expect it. How do you overcome discouragement and keep on going when it seems most bleak? How do you keep your faith and your smile and your hopes up? How do you keep on going?

pay attention to the way you feel. Experience your feelings, but don't wallow in them. See if there's worry, negative thoughts, tiredness - or any other feelings that pull you down. Then breathe into them, and as you exhale, breathe these negativities away, and imagine yourself as you'd like to be. Keep this vision close to your heart, and allow it to manifest for you when the time is right.

You can also meditate if you become discouraged. Become quiet and see if voices of encouragement will come through from the core of yourself. Sometimes, when your mind is still, the light can shine through from deep inside. You also need to move your body, exercise, rest and listen to whatever messages wish to come up from within.

About the Author

Coleman Christy TANO is a highly regarded psychologist, author, and expert in the field of Cognitive Behavioral Therapy (CBT). With a wealth of clinical experience and a deep commitment to advancing mental health, TANO has become a prominent figure in the integration of research and practical applications within the realm of psychological well-being.

As an accomplished author, TANO brings a unique blend of academic insight and real-world understanding to the forefront. Known for translating complex psychological concepts into accessible and actionable strategies, TANO's work resonates with both mental health professionals and individuals seeking personal growth.

With a passion for empowering others to unlock their mental potential, TANO's contributions extend beyond the pages of "Mastering Cognitive Behavioral Therapy." Through workshops, lectures, and continued research, TANO actively contributes to the evolution of therapeutic practices, advocating for the widespread adoption of evidence-based approaches to enhance overall mental health.

Coleman Christy TANO's dedication to the field, combined with a compassionate approach to mental well-being, makes "Mastering Cognitive Behavioral Therapy" not just a guide but a testament to TANO's commitment to fostering positive change and transformation in the lives of individuals and the broader mental health community.